ENGLISH ELECTRIC
CANBERRA

ENGLISH ELECTRIC
CANBERRA

Roland Beamont & Arthur Reed

LONDON
IAN ALLAN LTD

Dedication

To the designers, engineers, technicians and administrators at English Electric and the test pilots and aircrews of Warton, Samlesbury and Boscombe Down, and to the aircrews of the Royal Air Force and of the air forces around the world who have together made the name 'Canberra' famous in the history of aviation.

Cover:
Canberra aerobatics by an instructor of 231 OCU, RAF Bassingbourn. *MoD via RAF Wyton*

First published 1984

ISBN 0 7110 1343 8

Published by Ian Allan Ltd, Shepperton, Surrey; and printed by Ian Allan Printing Ltd at their works at Coombelands in Runnymede, England.

Acknowledgements

The task of recording events and personalities connected with nearly 40 years of pro-curement, development and in-Service experience of 22 variants of one type of air-craft has proved fascinating but formidable, and the authors have found it impossible in the space available to do justice to all the many thousands of skilled and dedicated pro-fessionals whose efforts have in total resulted in one of the most successful military aircraft of its time, even of all time.

Nevertheless it was felt that tribute should be paid to at least some of those carrying particular responsibility and a list of these is to be found at Appendix 5. To those not mentioned here or elsewhere in the text, who feel that they should have been, go the author's apologies, coupled with the thought expressed not infrequently by Freddy Page to frustrated members of the English Electric team — never mind, righteousness has its own reward!

The views and opinions expressed are the authors' own and do not necessarily reflect those of any other persons and authorities mentioned in the text.

Our grateful thanks are due to all those who have contributed memories, anecdotes, memorabilia and photographs. Among these have been Sir Frederick Page, Frank Roe, Ted Loveless, Ollie Heath, Bill Eaves, Ronnie Fox, Len Asher, Derek Hargreaves, Walter Shirley, Alec Johnston, Trevor Tarr, Eric Bucklow, Johnny Squier, Bob Mikesh, Dave Walker, Joe Sarginson, Allan Parkinson, Bob Fairclough, Air Commodore Geoffrey Cooper, James P. Woolsey, Derek Wood, Paul Jackson, David Dorrell, Gp Capt Ken Lovett (Commanding Officer) and Flt Lt Bob Latchem and others at RAF Wyton, Sqn Ldr Dave Cunliffe, the Air Historical Branch of the RAF, Gp Capt Alan Hollingsworth; and especially Chrys Butcher whose enthusiastic research and support throughout the project have been of the greatest value.

Contents

1 Introduction

In the history of aviation, of the many thousands of types of aircraft designed and built throughout the world for a multitude of purposes in war and peace, a relatively small number have proved to be so successful in combining performance, utility and maintainability with ease of operation and popularity with aircrew as to make them historically famous.

The first examples of this were undoubtedly the Avro 504 of 1914 and the Curtis 'Jenny' which together set for the first time standards of good, viceless controllability leading to the practical training of tens of thousands of pilots during World War 1 and on into the late 1920s.

In the 1930s the Hurricane, Spitfire and Douglas DC-2/DC-3 began their historic careers, followed during the war years of 1939-45 by the Lancaster, Mustang, Mosquito, B-17 Fortress, FW 190 and the Japanese Zero, each of which was the best in its class in the world. In the last months of that war the Me262 began to show that, as the world's first operational jet, it was also in this category of exceptional and memorable aeroplanes.

The immediate postwar period brought many prototype attempts at making good use of the newly available and powerful centrifugal and axial flow jet engines, but it was not until the emergence of the North American F-86 Sabre in 1948 and the Hawker Hunter in 1950 that the first of the 'classic' jet fighters appeared.

Similarly in the bomber field, the late 1940s produced a crop of twin and multijet prototypes in France, America and Britain of which the Boeing B-47 Stratojet and the English Electric A1 emerged as exceptional. It is the latter aircraft, later named Canberra, Britain's first jet bomber and the first design of a small team of specialist engineers and designers selected for the purpose and based initially in a deserted garage in the centre of industrial Preston at the end of World War 2, that is the subject of this book.

From its first public demonstration at the Farnborough display in 1949, the Canberra drew and held the attention of the aviation world. Here was a bomber which could out-manoeuvre all the fighters of the time and climb to 10,000ft and more above their ceiling; and one which was simple to maintain and a delight to fly. And it was British.

Right:
A B(I) Mk 12 for South Africa on production test from Samlesbury in 1963. *British Aerospace*

Left:
On test from Warton on 25 July 1950, the prototype B Mk 2, VX165, posed by the author for Charles Sims's camera (no telephoto lens!) in the tail turret of a Lancaster from RAE. Noteworthy are the internal 'blast protection' windscreen and absence of the final standard canopy rear fairing.
The Aeroplane

2 A Jet Bomber for the RAF

In 1937 the English Electric Company had begun to develop facilities at its heavy engineering and traction business at Preston in order to take part in the government scheme, following the Munich crisis, for the expansion of aircraft production as one of the Nuffield Shadow Factories. This took shape as a large production facility at Samlesbury airfield between Preston and Blackburn where it was well-sited to draw a workforce from both towns.

With massive assembly halls totalling 750,000sq ft of floor space, three wide runways and an extensive area of tarmac hardstanding and taxiways, this became the largest purpose-built aircraft assembly and test factory in the country; and by September 1939, at the outbreak of World War 2, it was heavily involved in the licensed production of Handley Page Hampden twin-engine bombers of which 700 were eventually built.

The transition from heavy locomotive engineering, in which English Electric Preston had been very successful under their redoubtable general manager Arthur Sheffield, to what was described as 'working with bent tin and alloy', was not achieved without considerable stresses and strains. Although aircraft construction was still 'engineering', it involved many disciplines which were strange to Preston and these had to be acquired quickly.

It was said that when the first Preston-built Hampden bomber was approaching completion the chief inspector at the Strand Road factory asked to see Sheffield and said, 'T'contract says here that the aircraft has to be test flown on completion — what are we going to do?' To which Arthur Sheffield is quoted to have replied, 'You'd better get a couple of your inspectors and send them on a pilots' course!'

In the event the Ministry of Aircraft Production arranged for selected RAF pilots to be attached for production test flying and these — Rose and Easedown — with occasional help from temporary Service pilots between them cleared 700 Hampdens and 2,145 Halifax four-engine bombers at Samlesbury by the end of the war.

The total of Halifaxes was greater than the number built by Handley Page themselves and it was this productivity, reaching 60 four-engine bombers a month at peak, coupled with the high standard of quality control achieved by English Electric at Preston, which led to their selection in 1944 as one of the companies short-listed with Vickers, Handley Page and Avro to develop the country's first jet bombers. At the same time, Hawker, de Havilland, Supermarine and Glosters were all developing jet fighters in their long-established and experienced design and experimental departments.

At this stage English Electric, which had had no aircraft design office since 1923, were faced with the urgent need to build up a team capable of handling this challenging task, and managing director George Nelson (the late Lord Nelson of Stafford) made the brilliant selection of W. E. W. Petter to form and lead the new team.

'Teddy' Petter had gained considerable experience as chief designer of Westland Aircraft, of Yeovil, where he had been responsible for the Whirlwind and Welkin twin-engined fighters. Although he had had success in that capacity he also had a reputation for eccentricity which was rapidly enhanced in the atmosphere of confrontation which soon developed between what were seen as 'Petter's newcomers' and the die-hard north-country engineers of Strand Road, Preston.

Petter had in fact a once-in-a-lifetime opportunity to form an entirely new design organisation to dove-tail into an existing powerful and successful production engineering company, with a potentially ready-made contract for one of the most fascinating and challenging projects of the period — the first British jet bomber. But it seemed a tall order in the circumstances and there were many loud voices protesting the impracticability of the project — not least from those areas of the aircraft industry which were already conscious of the severe cutbacks which would inevitably follow the onset of peace.

There would not be enough work to go round, it was said, so why encourage a new organisation to undertake work at an advanced technical level which would be beyond their experience and capability? This and many similar arguments were raised at the highest levels in a mounting attempt to discredit the project; and the news media, not slow to get wind of a 'controversial' story, lost no opportunity to raise doubts as to the Government's wisdom in placing so important a programme with a 'newcomer' to the aircraft industry. A well-known air correspondent of the time was widely quoted as referring to, 'this electrical bomber they are building up at Preston'!

Taking all this in their stride, Nelson and Petter screened and collected a small but strong team of specialists experienced in all the varied disciplines of military aircraft design with the emphasis on aerodynamics and design for high performance, for the new bomber was intended to be as fast as the new jet fighters and hopefully to fly much higher. A unique feature of the new team stemmed from this uncertainty because only those who were young, ambitious and not set in their ways were likely to be attracted to leave the stability of the big firms to take what must have seemed a considerable risk in joining an unknown organisation in the north-west.

Of course these circumstances also brought a risk of applications by some who could not make it elsewhere, but Petter was remarkably successful in screening out most of these and as the design organisation came together it was soon apparent that an exceptional team had been formed by early 1945, the year in which the prototype contract E3/45 was signed. (This was later changed to B3/45.) Many of the names from that time still served the Preston company more than 30 years later by which time it had been merged, consortiumed, nationalised and partly denationalised. Some of the people — such as D. Crowe, F. E. Roe, B. O. Heath and Ray Creasey — continued under Page's leadership to create the unparalleled record of technical success which followed at Warton on the subsequent programmes of the P1, Lightning, TSR2, Strikemaster, Jaguar and Tornado, as members of the divisional board of directors. This team effort was described in the 1970s by one well-known author as, 'the pre-eminent aircraft development team in Europe... not forgetting Hawker and Dassault.'

But in 1945 it was all just beginning and Teddy Petter, who had brought with him from Westlands some first thoughts on the layout for a light jet bomber replacement for the Mosquito, was now considering further options.

D. L. Ellis, a founder member of the team and specialist aerodynamicist who shared this area of responsibility with Ray Creasey, was recorded as saying, 'It was simple to sketch a wide range of convincing proposals on the basis of two or four (RR) centrifugal Nenes, or the axial engines under development by Armstrong Siddeley or Metrovic and to calculate the weapons bay and fuel for a given mission, but when it came to such basic questions as what shape you make the wing or where you put the engines, we were all stumped by the sheer profusion of possible answers. What's more we didn't have a high speed wind tunnel then.' This latter point was rectified by Ellis himself in 1949 when he designed for Warton Britain's first supersonic wind tunnel.

Petter was initially interested in a single-engine layout with a proposed big Rolls-Royce centrifugal engine delivering 13,000lb thrust at sea level, but he abandoned this when it became clear that with the fuselage full of engine there would be insufficient space for fuel and war load.

By July 1945 he had agreed with Rolls-Royce to go for a conventional twin-engine arrangement with a 6,500lb thrust RR axial initially identified as AJ65. Two of these engines would be buried in the wings and the fuselage would be available for fuel and war load.

Petter did not ignore the possible use of the then rapidly-becoming-fashionable wing sweep, but considered that with this level of thrust the specification could be met with a 'straight' wing of suitable thickness/chord ratio and that, 'sweeping back the wings and tail would have been pointless and would only have added weight'. It would also have reduced manoeuvrability, and a possible increase in performance from Mach 0.8 with a straight wing to Mach 0.9 with optimum wing sweep would not have been an overriding advantage. Greater speeds than this would have demanded more thrust than was potentially available in the timescale together with a thinner, heavier wing to deal with the suspected transonic drag rise; but that would need to be dealt with in the next generation of

9

aircraft after the B3/45 and the V-bombers that followed.

Late in 1944 Petter interviewed F. W. Page at Kingston in the process of engaging the founder members of his team. In 1982 Freddy Page, by then Chairman and Chief Executive of British Aerospace Aircraft Group and effectively head man of the British aircraft industry, recalled the Kingston occasion vividly.

At that time in 1944 he had been a senior aerodynamicist at the Hawker factory and had been responsible for the successful design and introduction of spring-tab controls to the Tempest fighter which had proved so successful in defence against the V1 flying bomb attacks that summer, and subsequently in the air fighting in the battle for Germany. This system had provided light and powerful aileron control to speeds above 500mph/IAS — experience which was to prove valuable to the Preston project.

Page recalled that Petter described the Westland ideas on a single engine in the fuselage layout, and that he took a general arrangement drawing home with him later, unrolled it on the floor and said to his wife Kathleen, 'If we do it, it won't look like that for sure because it won't work!'

He was already certain that to obtain the required high performance the weapons load

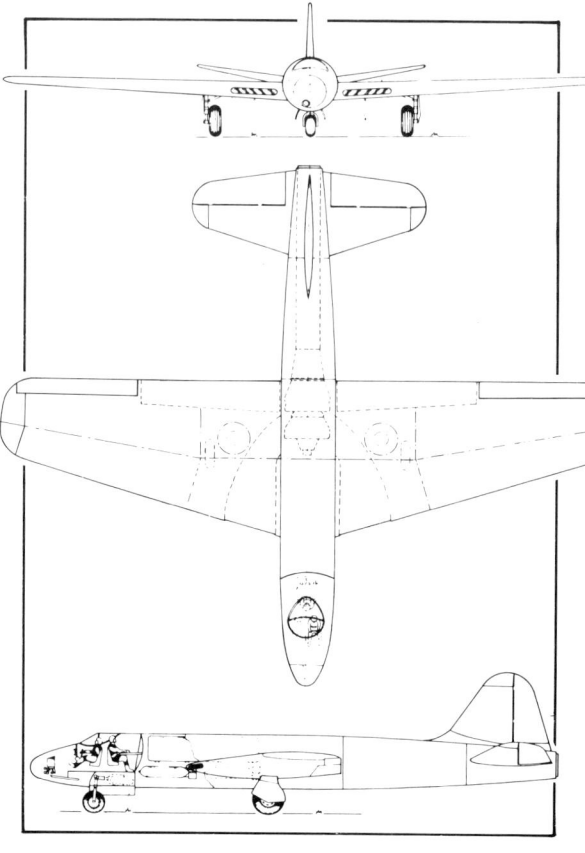

Above:
An initial single-engine configuration in 1945.
British Aerospace

Left:
Barton Motors — the birthplace of the Canberra design in 1945-48.
British Aerospace

Above right:
Twin-engine alternative 1945.
British Aerospace

Right:
General arrangement of the production B Mk 2.

would have to be carried in the fuselage, and that this would dictate that not one but two engines would have to be in or attached to the wing.

With remarkable insight Petter selected Page as his right-hand man and he left Hawkers in March 1945 to join English Electric where, in dreary makeshift offices in a requisitioned garage in Corporation Street, Preston, known locally as Barton Motors or 'TC' (it had been in use as a government training centre) he found that the team consisted of himself as Chief of Stress, Petter and one other — 'Harry' Harrison as Chief Engineer. Shortly afterward Don Crowe joined as Chief Draughtsman from Handley Page where his last post had been as design liaison engineer on the Halifax programme with English Electric.

Then began a period of intensive activity with the Ministry of Aircraft Production (MAP) on setting up procedures for recruiting a sufficient level of staff on which to base a contract; detailing of the contract; and establishing the channels for equipment supply.

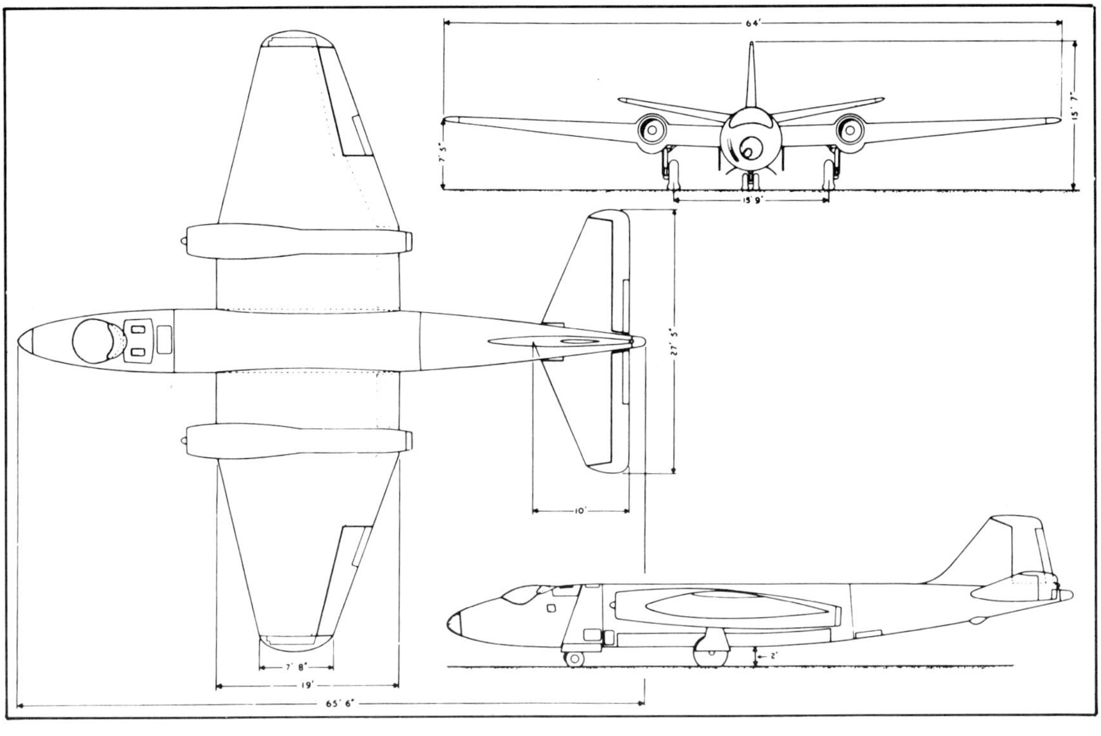

MAP policy was to preserve EEC's excellent wartime production record and to extend it with a new-design capability, but as the latter would take a number of years to form and mature there was a potential gap in

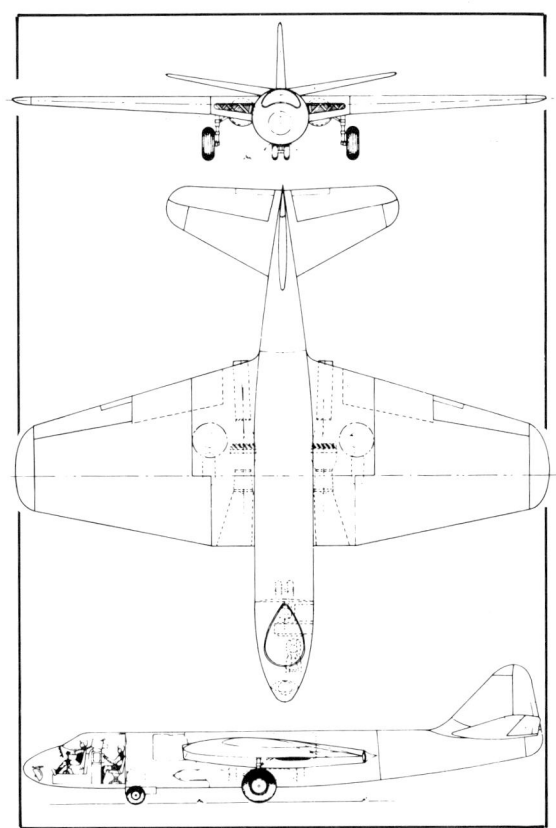

factory loading resulting from the end of Halifax production in 1945, and MAP placed a new production contract with English Electric for the licensed build of the DH Vampire jet fighter. This was to provide a valuable stepping-stone in works experience from heavy bomber construction to that of the lighter and closer engineering tolerance jet fighter, and 1,369 Vampires were built over the next four years.

Later in 1945 Page visited the Rolls-Royce factory at Barnoldswick with Petter for discussions with Adrian Lombard and Stanley Hooker who were engaged in the new AJ65 axial flow RR engine development.

This was followed by talks with Dr A. A. Griffiths, chief of jet engine design at RR Derby; and in May 1945 following a visit to Preston by N. E. Rowe, Director General of Technical Development at MAP, agreement was reached on a twin axial flow engine configuration in semi-buried wing nacelles.

At this time also Page's proposals for the undercarriage configuration were agreed and the first experimental contract was signed for several prototypes to B3/45 following submission of a technical brochure drafted in the nearby Victoria and Station Hotel.

Included in the proposal was provision for powerful longitudinal trimming by variable incidence tailplane of the anticipated strong Mach trim changes, and for spring-tab controls all round to cope with the proposed 500kts IAS design speed.

By the end of 1945 recruiting had been quite brisk with engineers and designers volunteering from industry, and some directed from other companies or as graduates from universities under the wartime direction-of-labour regulations still applying. So that in early 1946 some 260 employees formed the nucleus of the team, and included as leading specialists David (Dai) Ellis from Vickers as chief aerodynamicist; Ray Creasey, aerodynamics, from Vickers and R. (Bob) Hollock to take charge of prototype manufacture and the mock-up shops.

Ellis subsequently took a major part in the early flight development of the Canberra and of the design of the supersonic P1, and in the process contributed the design of the first supersonic wind tunnels to be built in this country, which commenced operation at Warton in the early 1950s.

Creasey provided the main inspiration for the successful aerodynamics of the B3/45 and went on to become a major authority in supersonic design. His work on the Canberra,

Top:
W. E. W. Petter at his desk at 'Barton Motors' in Corporation Street, Preston, 1947. *British Aerospace*

Above:
Dai Ellis at 'Barton Motors'. *British Aerospace*

Right:
'Strand Road' — the main English Electric factory in the heart of industrial Preston. *British Aerospace*

Below:
Don Crowe at 'Barton Motors'. *British Aerospace*

P1, Lightning, TSR2 and variable geometry projects, leading to the successful Tornado for NATO before his ultimely death at the age of 54, was a major contribution to the field of aeronautical engineering over the three decades from 1945.

An early recruit in 1946 was a graduate apprentice named Frank Roe who worked at 'TC' on the wing for the first prototype to the contract B3/45 for three flying prototypes and one structural test airframe. Roe remained in the mainstream of Canberra and Lightning development until becoming involved in factory management and administration leading to his eventual appointment as Managing Director of the division in 1981.

In late 1946 Petter began to consider the setting up of the flight test organisation that would be necessary for dealing with the test programme and in this area encountered one of the first of many confrontations with the established 'works' organisation.

The existing arrangements for production test flying of the sub-contract Vampire jet fighters were identical with those established for the Halifax and Hampden production runs in the period 1939 to 1945, and two company pilots, J. W. C. Squier and R. Blythe, were based at the Samlesbury factory airfield near Blackburn where they reported to the works superintendent, George Walker, and came under the overall control of Arthur Sheffield, the Works Manager at Preston.

Sheffield, who was in total charge of EEC Preston, was himself responsible to the English Electric Co board of directors chaired in London by Sir George Nelson (senior).

This arrangement did not suit Petter who saw 'development' as a distinct and separate activity from 'production' in every specialisation, and when he told Sheffield that he expected the pilots to report to him on the B3/45 experimental programme he received an uncompromising negative.

Not deterred for a moment by this, Petter set about recruiting a pilot for the post of 'chief experimental test pilot', and by December 1946 had reduced his search to a short list of two.

Of these, Sqn Ldr Tony Martindale was a serving officer test pilot at the Royal Aircraft Establishment at Farnborough who had achieved much experience and distinction in high speed diving trials to establish the absolute limits of control in compressibility. He had survived some remarkable experiences during these trials, including landing safely after the total loss of the propeller and reduction gear from a Spitfire in a vertical dive at over Mach 0.9 (90% of the speed of sound). Martindale was a qualified engineer and one of the most highly-rated test pilots at that time.

The other pilot under consideration was Wg Cdr Roland Beamont who in the seven years 1939-46 had completed three tours of fighter operations* in the RAF and two spells as an attached production and experimental test pilot at Hawker Aircraft. Immediately after World War 2 he had also had experience of jet fighter development with the Meteor IV at Glosters which had included much compressibility investigation and also preparation for the successful RAF 1946 attempt on the world's speed record, at speeds exceeding 600mph.

Both Petter and Page held strong views on the need for very close integration of the project test pilot with the design team on a shared-responsibility basis, and neither was interested in acquiring the at that time more traditional *prima donna* type for the important programme ahead.

Petter was attracted to the idea of Martindale's engineering background, but in a final discussion Page said that they, 'would have plenty of good engineers and what was needed was a test pilot with operational experience'. And so Beamont joined the team in May 1947.

*Including the Battles of France and Britain, nightfighting, Typhoon and Tempest ground attack, Tempest defence against VI flying bombs and airfighting over France and Germany from D-day onwards.

3 First Prototype

By 1947 a full-scale wood and cardboard mock-up of the B3/45 was in evidence in the old garage servicing bay at 'TC' and was the centre of design activity in the scheming of flying control runs, flaps and undercarriage, and in the positioning of equipment in the engine bays, the bomb bay and the cockpit. Crowe and Beamont spent much time in agreeing the inevitable compromises in the cockpit area between design requirements and operational acceptability.

This aircraft, which would be considerably larger than its predecessor the Mosquito, was intended to operate at or close to the speeds of current jet fighters, and so particular attention was given to achieving high quality flying control circuits with low levels of static friction.

The basic design philosophy of the wing was to have a symmetrical section with the centre of pressure well aft for a high usable Mach number, and that the inevitable buffet boundary which would be reached in level flight in this low-drag, high-powered aircraft would be made use of as an indication to the pilot of the limiting speed boundary.

Aileron and rudder would be mass-balanced, and aerodynamically horn-balanced up to approximately 80% of estimated requirements with the remainder provided by a spring tab system similar to that proved effectively on the Hawker Tempest and Sea Fury, to give suitably light stick forces; while the elevator would have over-static balance, horn balances and spring tabs.

At the anticipated speeds of 500kts IAS and Mach 0.8 plus there was some concern over the known difficulty with manual controls of accurate prediction of the relationship

Above left:
Meteor IV, EE545, taking off from Warton in 1948 on one of the investigations into the high altitude compressibility prior to Canberra flight testing. *W. Eaves*

Left:
Warton Aerodrome — the English Electric design and test centre, photographed in the late-1950s with five development Lightnings seen at the 'Southside' experimental flight shed. *British Aerospace*

Above:
Structural test airframe in the Warton mechanical test section in No 25 hangar, 1949. *British Aerospace*

Centre right:
VN799, the first prototype on preparation for flight in No 25 hangar during May 1949. *British Aerospace*

Bottom right:
Preparation for roll-out. *British Aerospace*

15

Right and below:
Roll-out, May 1949.
British Aerospace

between the aerodynamic coefficient B_1 (hinge moment) and B_2 (incidence), so it was decided to make the rudder horn balance area of wood to permit easy modification should flight testing prove this to be necessary. In the event this was seen to be a far-sighted precaution.

By the end of 1948 component assembly was almost complete partly at 'TC' and with the main components at Strand Road under the control of Bob Hollock, and Petter moved his design organisation into the deserted ex-USAF maintenance base at RAF Warton five miles down the Ribble estuary from Preston.

Beamont and W. (Bill) Eaves had been carrying out a Ministry contract trial at Warton in recent months to investigate high Mach number, high altitude manoeuvrability with a Ministry-loaned Meteor IV twin-jet fighter. This programme had gained valuable information on the loss-of-control phenomena beyond 80% of the speed of sound which at that time was still causing concern as it had since these characteristics had first been encountered by conventional propeller-driven fighters in combat from 1940 onwards. It was also a useful lead-in programme for Bill Eaves, experimental flight shed foreman, in preparation for the new prototype task ahead and it paved the way for setting up on a tight budget the barest facilities for the establishment of an experimental engineering and flight testing unit or 'Flight Shed' at Warton.

Early in 1949 final assembly and progressive system testing began in No 25 hangar at Warton. A major concern had been the late delivery of the flight engines due to development delays in the RA1 programme, and because of this as a safety measure the second prototype had been hurriedly re-engineered to take Rolls-Royce Nene centrifugals of 5,000lb

Top:
**Preparation for engine runs,
29 April 1949.** *British Aerospace*

Above:
**First engine run, May 1949. Bill
Eaves is wearing the hat.**
British Aerospace

Left:
**The original 'senior staff' at
Warton, May 1949. Left to right:
Crowe, Ellis, Harrison, Ellison,
Petter, RPB, D. Smith, Page,
Howatt.** *British Aerospace*

thrust. These necessitated bulged low-fineness-ratio nacelles to accommodate their bulky centrifugal shapes, and these were expected to incur drag and buffeting penalties; but they would ensure that at least one prototype would be flown in 1949.

However the flight-cleared pair of RA1s was delivered in March, and momentum increased rapidly.

The first E3/45 prototype, English Electric A1 serial number VN799, resplendent in all-over 'Petter' blue was unceremoniously rolled out of 25 hangar for engine runs on 2 May, and these were completed satisfactorily over the next five days.

Apart from some minor nosewheel 'shimmy' during taxying which began on 8 May, remarkably few unserviceabilities arose during these first tests, and it was soon possible for Beamont to begin the 'straight-hops' which he had called for to establish basic confidence in the flight controls before committal to the first flight.

In three of these 'hops' beginning on 9 May 799 was accelerated quickly at light load and with a fixed flap setting at 30° for max lift, through nosewheel lift at about 55kts to unstick at 75-80kts; on the first to check elevator 'feel' and response; on the second ailerons; and on the third the rudder.

The first two cases showed smooth and precise controllability, but on the third the rudder could be sensed only in limited displacements owing to the need to hold a straight line on Warton's narrow runway.

These straight 'hops' were remarkable in themselves as they confirmed the design predictions that this high performance bomber aircraft could easily be taken off, flown some 500yd, landed again and braked to standstill comfortably within the then 1,900yd Warton main runway, and without even overheating the brakes.

It was therefore in a mood of quiet confidence, in Flight Test at least, that the decision was made to go for first flight as soon as the appropriate weather conditions were available. These were defined as visibility 10 miles, no low cloud and less than half-cover, wind less than 20kts with less than 10kts crosswind component; and these conditions occurred on Friday 13 May 1949.

Below:
Flight certification. *British Aerospace*

CERTIFICATE OF SAFETY FOR FLIGHT.

M.A.P. Form 1090.

From :—

Inspector in Charge, A.I.D.,
The English Electric Co. Ltd.,
East Works, Preston, Lancs.

To :—

The English Electric Co. Ltd.,
Warton Aerodrome,
Nr. Preston, Lancs.

I HEREBY CERTIFY that the aircraft defined hereunder :—

Type	Engine(s).	Serial No. or Registration Mark.
B3/45 Prototype	RR.Avon R.A.2 A13/A617963 A14/A617964	VN.799.

has this day been inspected including the engine(s), the engine installation(s) and instruments and is in every way safe for the undermentioned flight(s) :—

Purpose of flight(s) Initial Taxying & Flight Trials in accordance with schedule of Flight Tests & Authority* Contract 5841/CB6(b). Design Certificate dated 5/5/49.
To take place

from WARTON Aerodrome with Mr. R.P. Beamont as Pilot.

NOTE.—Any alterations, repairs or adjustments made to this aircraft subsequent to the issue of this certificate renders it invalid, and no further flight may be made until the certificate is renewed.

Signed.

Date.

1 INITIAL TAXYING (LESS SEAT CHARGES)   7TH May 1949
3 INITIAL TAXYING (LESS SEAT CHARGES)   8 May 1949
2 TAXYING & HOPS (LESS SEAT CHARGES)   9TH May 1949
4 Hops   11 May 1949
5 Flight & Taxying   12TH May 1949
6 1st Flight   13TH May 1949

(*13706—7831) Wt/48659—3381 3M Pads 1/44 I.S. 700

*Contract, A. N. D., etc.

18

Left:
Preparation for taxying trials and 'hops'. *British Aerospace*

Below left:
First straight 'hop', 9 May 1949. *British Aerospace*

Below:
Second 'hop', 11 May 1949. *British Aerospace*

Bottom:
Final 'hop' — checking ailerons at about 85kts, 12 May 1949. *British Aerospace*

4   First Flight

Traditionally 'first flight' is an occasion of heightened interest at an aircraft factory, and this day was no exception at Preston. However it is doubtful if many English Electric personnel at that time had a full appreciation of just how momentous the occasion was.

This was to be the moment of truth in a number of hitherto controversial areas.

The design was the first major aircraft to originate from the Preston factory. It was Britain's first jet bomber, and the first in this country to be designed round axial flow jet engines.

It was the brain-child of the new team of designers whose future as individuals clearly depended upon its success, as did the future of the Preston production factory where the current Vampire contract ran out the following year.

It would in one step more than double the performance of RAF Bomber Command, and it would put Britain into the forefront of world aviation technology if successful.

If unsuccessful Britain would lose this classic opportunity to take the lead in jet bomber development, and the future of the Warton design team and possibly the whole Preston group would be in jeopardy; and there were very many pundits elsewhere in the aircraft industry, the RAF and the news media who seemed always ready to suggest that the project was doomed from the start owing to the 'inexperience' of English Electric.

There were also fortunately others in all these areas of sterner stuff who had staunchly maintained their belief in the potential of the formula of Petter's young team coupled with the sound and stalwart engineers of the English Electric factories in Lancashire.

So that it was with a very clear consciousness of these factors that the small flight test organisation at Warton made the final preparations on the morning of 13 May.

The weather, a vital factor, was excellent with a light northwesterly wind, no cloud and slightly hazy sunshine.

The by now routine '9 o'clock' meeting was finished in 15 minutes with the ruling that the flight would commence at 11am if no holding features occurred. A Vampire chase aircraft was ordered on standby from 10.45am at Samlesbury, to be flown by production test pilot J. W. C. Squier who was in later years as chief production test pilot to fly more than 3,000 Canberra test flights.

No specific arrangements had been made for viewing the event although it was expected that Petter and some of the designers and the flight shed staff would watch.

The main factories of Preston and Samlesbury would not be affected it was felt, as Vampire production should not be delayed by absent personnel.

Shortly before the '9 o'clock' meeting Petter in a final discussion with Beamont had suggested that as Friday 13th was not everybody's idea of a lucky day he would not argue with a day's delay, but Beamont was more than ready to fly.

At this point Petter characteristically disappeared from the scene, leaving it to those directly concerned with the job without interference for the next two hours and reappearing only to take the chair at the post-flight debriefing.

Final preparations proceeded in an almost unreal atmosphere of calm and confidence. Although new as a team every individual was experienced in his own area of expertise, and it was only at the last stage that one shortage of experience seemed marked, to the pilot at least — for it was to be his first prototype first flight also!

However Beamont's background in test flying had been quite progressive through production and experimental work, and any doubts he might have had had been dispelled by the ground tests of the past week, and especially by the short 'hops' which had already given a strong impression that this

Left, top to bottom:
Friday 13 May 1949, Warton, Lancs.

21

new aircraft was going to be smooth, easy and highly satisfying to fly; and so it proved to be.

By mutual agreement all spectator activity had been banned from the immediate vicinity of the prototype on the western end of the Warton tarmac, and when the pilot arrived the small group at the aircraft consisted only of Bob Hollock, development engineer in charge, Arthur Crombleholme, works inspector, 'Wilky' Wilkins, AID inspector and Bill Eaves with Bob Hothersall, airfield superintendent.

A few general words about nothing in particular, each having his own thoughts on this rather special occasion and then, Beamont recalled, as he settled into the cockpit Bob Hollock's hand came in through the door to wish him luck before the door was slammed closed and the good moment arrived — the cut-off from the outside world allowing total concentration on the job ahead.

The Avon engines started smoothly and quietly as they had through all the ground testing, and in this simple cockpit the few preflight checks of circuit breakers and fuel system tank selections were soon completed.

The chocks were waved away and, after the initial brakes test, 799 was taxied slowly down the short runway to join the main at the intersection and then back-track down to the east end (08).

There was no pressing time limit on this sortie — 799 could go when all was ready. The weather was good with a clear sky and a light NW breeze and good visibility. Warton Tower confirmed that Johnny Squier's Vampire was overhead and ready to join up for 'chase' observation, and suddenly there was nothing left to do but fly.

Nosewheel castoring was checked again and then the brakes as 799 was lined up on the centreline.

With 'you are clear take off' from the tower the Avons were brought smoothly up to full power against the brakes, checked for steady rpm, and jpt, oil pressure and temperatures and generator health and hydraulic pressure, and with the radio call 'rolling', the brakes were released.

This time with two hours' fuel on board the rate of acceleration was slightly slower, but nosewheel lift was still reached quickly at 65kts and the A1 became airborne in one smooth, progressive movement of the wheel at 80kts.

Throttling to keep speed down below undercarriage 'placard' a shallow climb attitude was established at 120kts and a small right rudder input checked. This gave initially correct response of left yaw but then the yaw suddenly increased with a jerk and apparently a sharp reduction of right pedal force. Centring the rudder returned the yaw to zero but jerkily with what semed like nonlinear pedal forces.

This would have to be investigated at a safe altitude, so as the rudder appeared to behave normally at or close to neutral, the undercarriage was retracted satisfactorily and the climb was resumed straight ahead until levelling off at 10,000ft off the coast at St Anne's.

Here in still air and with the Avons throttled down to maintain 220kts IAS it was immediately apparent that this was a remarkably smooth and quiet aeroplane. There appeared to be no airflow noise around the smooth lines of the nose fuselage and canopy; the aeroplane was in precise trim and remained so when the wheel and rudder pedals were released; and responses to small control inputs on elevator and aileron were positive and undramatic. It already felt like a thoroughbred to fly.

But with the Vampire close in to observe the result, a small rudder input confirmed a sensation of suddenly 'lumpy' fall-off in pedal force accompanied by an abrupt lurch in yaw.

Beamont called Squier in the Vampire and said, 'Did you see that wiggle?'; but nothing had been visible outside and Squier replied, 'No, but it looks damn nice!'

At this point, apart from the rudder problem the aircraft was functioning well and Beamont was tempted to continue with the planned investigation of low-speed handling, but as the rudder was now suspect and could result in complications in the event of a flameout or other failure with one of these equally new and untried engines, the flight was cut short and after a slow-down to assess controlability at 90kts to establish a practical approach condition, 799 entered a slow descent back towards the Warton circuit.

Joining downwind south of the airfield over the River Ribble and lowering the undercarriage which gave three comforting green lights, Beamont recalls a moment of realisation that this was indeed a remarkable aircraft with firm, sure characteristics which seemed to almost invite the pilot to leave it to fly itself quietly home; and it was with a sense of real pleasure that he felt its precise responses as the final turn was rolled out on to the approach with only gentle guidance required from the pilot.

At about 200ft and 100kts with 700yd to go to the runway threshold a patch of turbulence rocked the aircraft and instinctive pilot corrections resulted in holding the approach accurately in pitch and roll, but the rudder non-linearity appeared again causing a brief and disquieting lurch in yaw.

By this time in otherwise perfect control the approach was continued down to begin an easy flare at about 30ft which resulted in a gentle touchdown at 85kts followed by progressive lowering of the nosewheel into contact and a roll-out to standstill in about 800yd with gentle, effective braking.

It had been a smooth, quiet, undramatic event, and it was only then that the pilot became conscious that the greenhouse effect of the 'blown' one-piece canopy was becoming uncomfortable in the May sunshine.

Taxied back to its corner of the otherwise deserted tarmac 799 swung round and shut

down engines. The small ground party gathered round the hatch as the pilot climbed out. North-country reticence ensured against any recognition of abnormality in the occasion: 'So there were no systems snags — oh aye, why should there be!' With a shrug the tractor was hitched on and the all-blue prototype towed off to the hangar almost as if nothing had happened.

In Petter's office the atmosphere was more obviously relieved, but still professional.

The pilot's report was listened to in silence until he observed that the rudder hinge moment non-linearitly 'felt like overbalance', and this brought a quick response of 'it couldn't be' from someone in the design office. But Petter quickly countered that it could well be overbalance and that no-one should jump to conclusions.

Beamont said that apart from the rudder the prototype was in excellent shape to continue, but that he felt that a positive decision and some modification action was needed in respect of the rudder before Flight 2.

Below:
Possibly the only in-flight photograph of VN799 with the original rudder shape. *British Aerospace*

5   Flight Development

By the end of the day on 13 May the decision had been taken to investigate the rudder problem by ad hoc modifications to reduce the horn balance area in stages.

The first of these was flown on 18 May and was successful in restoring conventional rudder response and 'feel'. General handling was investigated up to 420kts and to 15,000ft and control and stability was assessed as excellent, but a vibration problem was encountered at speeds above 400kts IAS.

This was described by Beamont as 'heavy tramping — mostly vertical and at about 6-10cps', and he said that it felt like flutter.

As this would need careful investigation eventually it was decided to explore the flight envelope within a 'safe' 400kts IAS limit and on the next day, 19 May, 799 reached 20,000ft and Mach 0.77 at which point some moderate 'snaking', or short-period, low-amplitude direction oscillation occurred.

It was confirmed that this condition was a function of Mach number and that it appeared at any altitude at around Mach 0.77.

Returning to the flutter case on 26 May a severely limiting condition was encountered at 420kts at 10,000ft on flight 7; and on flight 8 the next day with vibrograph sensors fitted, the oscillation was measured at 8cps vertical with some 24cps and identified as incipient elevator flutter.

On 31 May Beamont flew with Dai Ellis in the navigator's seat to gain a practical experience of this phenomenon; and with the confidence of nine test flights behind him he took 799 directly to the onset of the '8 cycle' at 10,000ft. Holding it in the violent buffeting vibration for long enough to impress his passenger he throttled back and slowed 20kts back into smooth flight. 'What did you think of it Dai?' he said. 'Christ!' said the voice from the back.

'Well' said RPB, 'we'll just go and have another look . . .' But with firm decision the voice from the back said, 'I think the best place to investigate that is on the ground!'

The prototype was laid up after flight 11 on 1 June until 5 July for modifications to the elevator horns and mass balances, and to produce a 'production' shape for the revised rudder horn. Work was also carried out in this period on plans to eliminate the 'snaking' characteristic, and when flying began again it

Left:
Altimeter calibration runs past Warton Tower with modified rudder, June 1949.
British Aerospace

Above right:
1949 — the first air photograph, here closing in on the Lancaster. Note modified rudder, but original dorsal fin area. *IPC Press*

Right:
The clean lines are emphasised.
IPC Press

introduced a period of intensive and successful handling tests aimed at establishing a suitable standard for a public debut at the Farnborough Show in September and, of greater
importance, the achievement of a satisfactory
configuration for offering for evaluation by
Boscombe Down soon after Farnborough.

Progress was rapid and in 36 flights
between 6 July and 31 August handling
clearance was achieved over the whole initial
design flight envelope, the '8-cycle' flutter

case responding well to the elevator modifications and the 'snaking' being traced to wake
turbulence behind the canopy and cured by a
simple fairing.

During these tests 40,000ft was exceeded
(to 42,000ft) for the first time on 11 August,
and MO.8 on 12 August. Then on 31 August
the initial design speed of 470kts IAS was
achieved at 4,500ft giving the required
margin of 20kts over the proposed initial
Service limit of 450kts IAS.

Above:
Coming in towards the stern turret of the Lancaster.
British Aerospace

Right:
Close-up. Note original 'safety' windscreen inside the canopy.
British Aerospace

Below right:
Breaking formation. RPB has removed his helmet owing to the heat of the greenhouse-like cockpit. *IPC Press*

Above:
Ray Creasey, founder and leader of the Warton Aerodynamics tradition until his death in 1976, aged 54. *British Aerospace*

In all of this flying smooth, responsive and stable handling qualities were apparent and with its moderate wing loading and reserves of power the manoeuvrability still available at above 40,000ft was for that time astounding.

It was now clear that authority would be obtained to go to Farnborough but it was not until the last week in August that flying time could be devoted to working up a demonstration routine, although there had been considerable discussion about it, as a result of which Beamont had concluded that while no-one was going to say that a bomber aircraft

should be aerobatted, there was no design reason why the full capabilities in terms of roll rate and 'g' should not be used in conjunction with the lowest practical wing loading and the good power-to-weight ratio.

So on 22 August on the way back from some high M handling at 40,000ft, full rolls, rolls-off loops and full loops were investigated and found to be smooth and straightforward, though needing some muscle power where speeds above 350kts were necessary.

During the next week in a further 10 flights a six-minute demonstration routine was practised, and then 799 was flown to Farnborough on 4 September resplendent in renewed and highly polished overall blue finish.

By this time the word had got around, and at Warton particularly there had been some voices protesting that the prototype should not be 'risked' in this way and that 'aerobatics' were not suitable for bombers, etc. However Teddy Petter remained aloof from these attitudes and expressed the view that his chief test pilot would know best how to present the new aircraft.

This provided the needed atmosphere of confidence and with the enthusiastic support of Dai Ellis and of flight test engineer Dave Walker who was to fly in the demonstrations as test observer, Beamont flew to Farnborough on the Sunday without revealing his demonstration intentions, and with a fully serviceable aircraft all was ready for the opening day, Monday 6 September.

With the initial RA1 engines giving only 6,000lb thrust each and substantially less than the projected production RA3s, it was not considered 'cheating' to fly with a low fuel load of 3,000lb distributed in the main fuselage tanks, and this led to an unexpected complication.

At this early stage engineering tests of the installed fuel system had not completed 'free surface area' checks of how far the tanks could be run down before fuel pressure was lost.

Then as briefed, 799 was taxied out for the first demonstration using the last of the fuel in the rear tank to ensure that the demonstration could be flown within CG limits solely on the two forward tanks with ample fuel in them.

Left:
799 climbing steeply after take-off in less than half the Warton runway on an early test flight in the summer of 1949. *British Aerospace*

With all eyes on it the sleek blue jet turned to line up for take off in front of the control tower — and then the port engine stopped! RPB was already in the process of selecting the forward tanks and hoped that this would restore power, but it did not and the unburnt fuel from the 'good' tanks now flowing through the engine to the hot tail pipe caused an enormous cloud of grey smoke!

Now there was a dilemma, because although the crew fully understood what had happened there was no immediate means of restarting the external battery starter engine, and Beamont called the tower to explain and ask for a later slot. This was confirmed and the next aircraft called forward for take off, but while all this was going on Petter, appalled at this apparently dramatic technical incident, leapt over the crowd barrier and ran across the runway in use to his ailing prototype! There ensued some hard words from the authorities and also between Petter and the engineers when the former gave orders for, 'all the tanks to be filled up'. Beamont said that it had been his mistake not to change tanks earlier and that he was happy with the planned loading and Joe Sarginson, the design office engineer in charge, took the responsibility of ignoring Petter's order and not altering the fuel state. Subsequently Petter was magnanimous in writing to Sarginson saying, 'You kept you head when others failed — take 3 days' leave'.

Meantime the opening day display of Farnborough 1949 continued in the hot sunshine with many fascinating new prototypes including the first public appearance of the world's first jet airliner, the DH Comet flown by John Cunningham; and then it was time for the last item.

This time with no problems 799 rolled into its take-off run, leapt into the air after less than 700yd, was held down until reaching 200kts and then entered a 45° banked climbing turn to the left. Reversing this to the right and in a dumb-bell turn through 800ft over Laffan's Plain the blue jet bomber was brought back down the runway at 100ft at full power and pulled up vertically when passing the tower at 400kts into a half-loop followed by a 45° downward roll through 220° to dive with power off back to the western boundary to a left turn in for a 360° roll along the runway from 100ft to 500ft.

Then left into a vertical bank around the north boundary, pulling the turn tight at 4g and 250kts to continue round immediately in front of the crowd before rolling out to the east and pulling up into a wing-over, dropping the speed to 150kts and lowering the undercarriage while turning left-handed over the crowd to come back in a low left turn to line up with the runway just short of the tower at low speed, rocking the wings.

Throttles to full power, undercarriage up and then a dumb-bells wing-over to the west to come back for the final item — pulling up from 380kts at 100ft in front of the tower to roll out at the top of a half-loop, lowering undercarriage and bomb doors for a high rate of descent left-spiral down to land. Then drama again!

As the bomb doors opened with their normal roar and turbulence at about 160kts the aircraft gave a lurch and a number of instruments flickered.

Dave Walker said, 'My instrumentation has gone' and RPB said, 'So have my starboard engine instruments'. Then Farnborough tower — 'B3/45 you are dropping pieces!'

Above:
Vintage SBAC display. The English Electric B 1 is prepared for its public debut at Farnborough, 1949.

Behind can be seen, from left to right, the prototypes of the Vickers Viscount, de Havilland Comet and Armstrong Whitworth Apollo.

Left:
EE Co directors and the Warton support party at Farnborough in 1949. H. G. Nelson, 'Joe' Sarginson, Hart, Petter, Sir George Nelson, Crombleholme, S. Graham, Davenport (R.R.).
British Aerospace

Below:
799 begins its take-off on the opening day.

RPB continued the spiral descent to position for a one-engine landing if necessary, but then established by throttle response that the starboard engine was not dead although its instruments were.

The approach was continued to a smooth landing with the tower coming up with the information that, 'You are trailing wires and things from under your fuselage'. It was apparent to the crew that something drastic had happened to the test instrumentation pack that was mounted in the bomb bay and when 799 was stopped discreetly on the taxiway behind the wood on the northwest side of the airfield out of sight of the crowd, Dave Walker opened the hatch and dived underneath. He confirmed that the instrumentation box had disappeared and all that

was left was a handful of wires, but there was no other damage.

The flight instruments were made good overnight and the decision made reluctantly to continue the demonstration week without test instrumentation, since a new pack would take time to make up.

Reactions to the first demonstration were immediate and strong. The impact on the aviation world was marked enough but that on the display control committee even more so. Beamont was called before them on the following morning and told to 'tone down' his display. In querying what that meant no positive answer was forthcoming, so he asked directly if the display had been considered dangerous. 'Well no,' he was told, 'but just cool it'.

Right:
799's undercarriage coming up on its first Farnborough display.

Below:
The Canberra landing past the president's tent at the end of its opening display, 6 September 1949. *D. Woods*

It transpired that one member of the committee with heavy responsibility in aviation insurance had said that, 'he had never seen anything like it and wasn't prepared to cover it'. However the senior test pilot member, 'Mutt' Summers, Chief Test Pilot of Vickers, satisfied himself in subsequent discussion with Beamont that the aircraft was in fact at all times being flown within its proved safety margins; and the remainder of the week's demonstrations were flown to the same routine and without incident, and when 799 flew back to Warton on the final Sunday with Joe Sarginson in the back seat it was obvious that the new aircraft had created a considerable stir in the aviation world.

The editorial of *Aviation Week*, the leading North American aviation journal, summed up some years later:

'Salute to the Canberra

Technological progress is so rapid in aerospace that it is only rarely that an aircraft design endures in active service for several decades. The Douglas DC-3 was the great durable workhorse of the transports, and it involves small risk to speculate that the English Electric Canberra twin-jet bomber will occupy a similar niche among combat aircraft. After 23 years of operations under 16 flags and through four wars, the durable Canberra is still producing new variants and is programed in various air forces for operational use to nearly the end of this century.

'The Canberra design was conceived in 1944 by that brilliant eccentric, W. E. W. ''Teddy'' Petter, as Britain's first jet bomber and eventually evolved into the British Air Ministry Specification B3/45. Petter later designed the Lightning and Gnat interceptors and died tragically on a mountain crag in Switzerland. The Canberra mockup was created in a brick garage in downtown Preston, a venerable Lancashire mill town. The first prototype flew in May, 1949, piloted by the man who was destined to play a unique role in its development success — Roland P. Beamont.

'Some four months later, the Canberra and its astonishing performance first burst on an unsuspecting aeronautical world at the Farnborough flying display of the Society of British Aircraft Constructors. This was the first Farnborough this reporter ever covered, and we quote with pardonable pride our evaluation of "Bee" Beamont's skilful display of his remarkable mount (AW&ST Sept. 19, 1949, p. 12).

"Biggest military surprise of the show was the English Electric Co. sky-blue Canberra jet bomber. US observers were not impressed with the Canberra's straight wing and somewhat conventional configuration on the ground. But in the air, the combination of test pilot R. P. Beamont and the 15,000lb thrust from the two axial Avons made the Canberra behave in spectacular fashion. Its speed range from 500mph to less than 100mph was ably demonstrated by Beamont, who followed his high-speed passes on the deck with an approach using full flaps, gear down and bomb bay doors open that slowed the Canberra to less than 100mph. At this speed he rocked the big bomber violently with the ailerons to show the full control available as it approached stalling speed.

"Beamont whipped the bomber, designed to carry a 10,000lb bomb load, around the deck like a fighter, flying it through a series of slow rolls, high-speed turns and remarkable rates of climb.

"The Canberra was originally designed for radar bombing at around 50,000ft, but Beamont's demonstration convinced many Britishers that the new bomber may prove to be another Mosquito in its versatility at everything from low-level attack through night fighting to high-altitude bombing."

'This was the first of the countless demonstrations by "Bee" Beamont that sold the Canberra to 15 other air forces including the US Air Force (B-57) and racked up more than $240 million in sales with the cash register still ringing. Petter's concept of a very low wing loading, very strong structure (it could take 5g) and simplicity of systems for easy maintenance and high utilisation under field conditions has stood the test of time and new technology.

'The Canberra was revolutionary for its day (it doubled the speed of bomber forces), yet it has remained contemporary with the addition of new technology in powerplants and avionics.

'Between 1951 and 1958, the Canberra set a score of world records, of which 13 still stand today. Perhaps the most notable was the first double crossing of the Atlantic in a single day, on 26 August 1952. It flew from Aldergrove in Northern Ireland to Gander, Newfoundland, and back covering, 4,144 stat miles in 10hr 3min, averaging 411.99mph. Spectators at 18 subsequent Farnboroughs enjoyed its performance. The Canberra last flew at Farnborough in 1970 displaying the livery of the Argentine navy.

'The Canberra sprouted many variants and played many roles. It fought the Egyptians in the 1956 Suez campaign, was used in both India-Pakistan wars and until recently was fighting in USAF insignia in Vietnam. It has functioned as a drone target for guided missile tests, chase plane for the Concorde, close support bomber, night intruder, photo recon, and as a lowly tug towing gunnery targets. With great stretches of wingspan added and some 45,000lb thrust of powerplants installed, it became the RB-57F and sailed serenely over Russia and China at attitudes of more than 80,000ft on undisturbed reconnaissance missions and sniffed the nuclear debris hurled to those altitudes by weapons tests.

'A total of 1,376 Canberras were built in England, the US and Australia. In addition to the many modifications and variant programs with USAF models, some 90 Canberras have been modernised in England and resold to foreign air forces where their rugged simplicity and versatility still make them attractive. In addition, another round of modifications is producing new versions for both the Royal Navy and Air Force that will add at least another decade of operational use. . .

'Performance of the Canberra in all its variants over more than two decades has assured it a well-carved niche in the galaxy of great combat aircraft. The Canberra success is also another fine example of what a relatively small but highly competent team of design engineers and engineering test pilots can accomplish with a minimum of interference from the requirements of bureaucracy. — **Robert Hotz**'

Above:
VX165 demonstrates at Farnborough, 1950. *D. Woods*

Nevertheless despite the gratifying euphoria, it was realised at Warton that the work of getting this new aircraft into a condition in which the RAF could make good use of it had only just begun, and that while helpful to the vitally important establishment of confidence in the project, the current wave of interest was based more on the newness of the concept of high jet power with low wing loading than on any magical breakthrough in design technology. The B3/45 was a good, honest, 'clean' and amenable aircraft and using this experience for display flying to advantage the full potential of this configuration was exploited over the next few years. It was soon realised that within the strictly limited time available at displays of six to seven minutes, and often as little as five minutes from take-off to landing, the wrong thing to do was to wind it up to limit speed flypasts as was popular with the jet fighters.

Far better to keep the speed down except for one high-speed run, and spend the rest of the allotted time using the tremendous low-speed manoeuvrability balancing induced drag as required with frequent bursts of maximum power to keep as close inside the airfield boundary and therefore as close to the spectators as possible.

In this process and as experience was gained, further refinements proved practical such as looping plane entries down to 320kts, and 'inside the boundary' vertically banked turns at less than 200kts sustained with the roar of full Avon power.

Its first overseas showing was with fourth prototype VN850 and was received with acclamation at the Paris Show at the newly-opened Orly airport on 11 and 12 June 1950, as it was again at the Belgian Show at Antwerp on 24 and 25 July; and for the next four years the breaking into of intensive test programmes to provide aircraft for Press, Service mission and customer demonstrations became a significant though often irksome factor in the Warton programme.

These frequent commitments brought much opportunity for practice and further refinement of what became widely known as 'Canberra style' demonstrations, and when in September 1954 the first prototype of the last bomber variant, B(1) Mk 8 VX185,* was shown at the Farnborough Show, the aviation Press described it as 'the superb Canberra B8 giving what was probably one of the finest ever displays of a military aircraft'.

Despite all this the qualities which resulted in this level of fame were not that the Canberra was exceptionally aerobatic. It was, recalls Beamont, docile and completely vice-less so that it could be flown safely to its limits of performance and manoeuvrability and at very low speed by comparison with the minimum manoeuvre speeds of all other contemporary jets. Thus, if the pilot was prepared to fly slow demonstrations and had well-developed biceps, for this was still a bomber aircraft and no delicate fighter, then the Canberra could get more into the standard five minutes than most other jets and could continue to do so in atrocious weather when other aircraft were limited.

It was this uncomplicated ease of operation and maintainability with its unusual flexibility of roles which led to the continued world-wide use of Canberras for the next 30 years.

Converted from the Mk V prototype for evaluation of the Mk 8 configuration.

6   Management Crisis

By late 1949 with development well advanced and production in sight a crisis occurred in the English Electric management. Relations between the Preston engineering works at Strand Road and the design 'newcomers' at Warton, which had been strained from the beginning of the programme, had deteriorated into what amounted in some areas to interdepartmental warfare by the early 1950s.

The greatly respected and successful Preston General Manager, Arthur Sheffield, was widely quoted as saying that, 'What that carnival lot at Warton want is English Electric Aviation in ten-foot letters over the main gate at Warton, but they'll never bloody get it!'

Petter on the other hand could see no future for his design organisation unless he could have full autonomy at Warton including his own experimental engineering department, in order to put a stop to the endless in-fighting between his designers and the production-orientated Strand Road works. There was in fact fault on both sides.

By early 1950 with the demanding P1 supersonic fighter programme then building up on top of the wave of Canberra success, Petter brought the issue out into the open by making his continued service with the company conditional on a separate administration for Warton and an experimental shop there, both to be under his control.

There is no doubt that company chairman Sir George Nelson (the late Lord Nelson of Stafford) regarded this as a potential disaster and tried desperately to prevent the loss of Petter who was at that time already regarded as one of the top aircraft designers in the country; but Nelson was evidently unable to achieve a compromise acceptable to both sides and he refused Petter his experimental department.

From December 1949 Petter had ceased to take an active part at Warton and F. W. Page took over the day-to-day management until in March 1950 Petter resigned and Page was appointed as his successor.

This was a traumatic upheaval at the point of major success as despite his detractors, of which this strange and strong personality had many, Petter had created a powerful team spirit at Warton which was closely dependent on its leader.

Petter, in leaving to take charge of Folland Aircraft Ltd, made it known that he would be happy for some of his specialist colleagues to join him, and this potential instability so disturbed the Ministry of Supply that Sir George Nelson visited Warton to attempt to persuade key members of the 'monthly' staff to sign fixed-term contracts which none of them had been offered before! Some signed up and some did not, and a few left Warton to join Petter at Hamble including Harrison from the production design office and Walker from flight test.

But the initial storm was ridden and Page began a commitment which carried Warton from success to success over the years from 1950 to 1982. In that year he was, as Chairman and Chief Executive of British Aerospace Aircraft Group, technical head man of the aircraft industry and as such still in overall charge of affairs at the Warton Division which had by then become by far the largest and most successful aircraft design and production centre in the country.

This did not come easily at first, and the initial strains of restabilising the Warton situation while maintaining firm control of the Canberra and the new P1/Lightning supersonic programmes resulted in a period of ill health for Page. During his illness the quality of the Warton team was demonstrated to the full by the able way in which senior specialists such as Creasey, Crowe, Ellison, Dickson, Heath, Roe and many others, rose to the occasion and kept these vital activities on schedule until Page recovered.

It was a time of uncertainty and there were many who expressed doubts as to the future of Warton, but few if any of these doubters were members of the team itself.

7 The B3/45 Prototypes

During the evolution years of the A1 from 1945 to 1947 it became apparent that the radar bombing system which had been a key design point for this high altitude, high speed Mosquito replacement, was falling far behind in development.

Concurrently the 'cold war' international tension with Russia was already creating a rearmament atmosphere, and in order to avoid delaying introduction of this new-regime aircraft a far-sighted decision was taken to issue a new requirement B5/47 for a revised version of the B3/45 with provision for a visual bombing system with a third crewman as bomb-aimer. Four prototype A1s had been ordered in 1945, and the second of these was to have two 5,000lb thrust Rolls-Royce Nene centrifugal flow engines as an insurance against delays to the test programme which might have occurred owing to late delivery of the axial flow Avons which were themselves encountering development problems.

There were many at the time who doubted the viability of visual bomb-aiming from 40 or 50,000ft, and these doubts developed into strong conviction when the aircraft subsequently entered service to an extent that there was much talk at RAF staff levels of the aircraft being 'operationally useless'. Luckily as so often happens, at user level in the squadrons appreciation of the exceptional qualities of the aeroplane quickly developed and ideas were put forward as to how best to adapt it to different roles.

Other roles had already been planned such as the photo-reconnaissance PR3 and the dual trainer T4, but few at least in 1947 could have foreseen that in one of its main and most effective activities in the future this very high-altitude aircraft would be employed in the structurally demanding role of low-altitude interdictor, and would use up its fatigue life in so doing in half the planned timescale.

But in 1947 this was all in the future, and in an atmosphere of mounting world tension and of increasing concern about the relative shortcomings of the outdated Mosquitos and Lincolns still equipping Bomber Command, a production order was placed in March 1949 for the B Mk 2 and PR3 developments of the basic A1. Totalling 132 aircraft the contract included 90 B5/47 bombers, 34 PR31/46 reconnaissance aircraft and eight T2/49 dual control trainers.

Below:
The four prototype B Mk 1s at Warton, December, 1951.
British Aerospace

A quantity production order on this scale was unusual before first flight even of a prototype, but when this was accomplished successfully with VN799 two months later the programme moved forward with a surge of confidence at Ministry, factory and Service levels which became a sustained hallmark of the Canberra operation throughout the next 30 years.

The four prototypes to the original B3 contract were completed and all made their first flights in 1949. The first, VN799 in May, had completed 50hr testing before the Farnborough Show in September and 100 hours by the end of the year, and had established the basic handling standards required for production. In the process it achieved provisional official acceptance at its first Boscombe Down preview trial in October where RAF test pilots Wg Cdr Davies, Sqn Ldr Saxelby and Flt Lt Callard reported very favourably and pronounced themselves in full agreement with the briefing of the English Electric Co.

Little more than five months after first flight VN799 was flown to Boscombe Down on 27 October for these 'preview' trials on which so much depended, and the company team's report on the initial reactions of the B Squadron test pilots indicated that no major criticisms seemed likely to emerge.

'Report on the first week of Service trials on VN799 at RAF Station, Boscombe Down

VN799 was delivered to Boscombe on 27 October, and the remainder of that day and the whole of the following day were occupied with weighing, general servicing, and discussion with Mr Wills and his technical staff, and with the pilots of B Squadron.

'The machine was serviceable at 10 o'clock on the morning of 29 October and three familiarisation sorties were made with B Squadron test pilots.

'The latter were seated on the folding seat and they reported it to be uncomfortable but extremely useful. Wg Cdr Davies (commanding B Squadron) particularly recommended the retention of a seat of this description as being ideal for conversion and general familiarisation on the type.

'The main criticism on discomfort was based on the fact that in its present position the passenger has to sit against the sharp corner of the radar panel support pedestal. Both this and the other criticism, that the seat is too low, could be covered by redesigning for a more forward position. This would in turn allow the use of a pilot-type parachute where this is not at the moment possible; the pilots in this instance wore observer-type harness and stowed a parachute under the seat.

'Cockpit drill, engine and airframe limitations, take-off procedure, stalling, engine stopping and relighting, single-engine handling, low and high speed characteristics and approach and landing were all demonstrated to each pilot in the course of the flight. Each pilot was given 25 minutes' flying, and after the flight the aircraft was refuelled at once and the first pilot sent off solo.

'Three pilots were put off during the afternoon and their impressions were recorded immediately after flying as follows:

'Wg Cdr Davies — Flight 1

He was generally very impressed. He criticised the position of the tail trim switch on the left side of the wheel and suggested that it must be repositioned on the right. His first impressions of longitudinal trim control by switch were not good and he said that the system could be dangerous if misused, but he agreed that this was a case of first experience without a manual trim wheel.

'He praised the smoothness and harmony of ailerons and elevator, but criticised the lightness of the rudder about neutral, though only from the point of view of spoiling harmony. He was most impressed with the general ease of control at all speeds, the viceless stall, the simplicity of take-off and landing, and with the very low cabin noise level.

'Sqn Ldr Saxelby — Flight 1

This pilot has a reserved nature but was visibly impressed upon landing. He liked the tail trim control and switch, but would like to see it on the right side of the wheel. He was most impressed by the general qualities of control response and harmony, by the speed and rate of climb and by the quietness and general apparent lack of effort with which the aeroplane flies in all conditions. He commented that without prejudice to future developments it is "the finest machine I have ever flown".

'Flt Lt Callard — Flight 1

This pilot was also very impressed upon landing, but had no specific comments to make beyond the fact that he had experienced a first-class example of "classic snaking" by applying ailerons at 400kts; and then went on to say that it was damped out in 4/5 cycles, rudder free. There was no doubting his general enthusiasm however particularly with regard to the simplicity of control at low speeds.

'During the morning of 30 October the aircraft was unserviceable and the bleed valve and control units were changed on the starboard motor. Flying began again in the afternoon as follows:

'Wg Cdr Davies — Flight 2

He climbed the machine to 20,000ft and carried out handling tests to 0.78M and to 2g at 0.6M. He commented that the machine handled "marvellously" under these conditions. He was generally even more impressed than with his first flight, and agreed now that electric trimming becomes more acceptable with practice. He raised doubts of the flat approach characteristics, especially with regard to training and night flying, but this may again be a case of becoming used to the type of machine. He referred frequently to buffeting from flaps at 140kts, but admitted that any tendency to buffet fades below 120kts. He did not like the nose-up moment at 140kts with full flap, but pointed out that this was not intended to be a serious criticism.

'Sqn Ldr Saxelby — Flight 2

He carried out low speed investigation up to 15,000ft and was again well pleased in every way. He regarded the controls as remarkably well-harmonised and again had no special criticism but was full of praise for the outstanding ease of control and stable characteristics.

'Flt Lt Callard — Flight 2

He flew the machine to 0.79M and stated that he experienced no compressibility symptoms at 15,000ft. This would appear to have been a misreading of the Mach meter. He criticised strongly the nose-up trim moment with flaps down at 140kts and stated that the aircraft will stall stick-free at this condition, which is of course correct. He had no other criticisms.

'At the end of the day's flying all three pilots were unanimous on the poor vision properties of the canopy into sun and haze. All three chose downwind landing runs rather than up-sun.

'The aircraft was unserviceable on the morning of 31 October owing to a u/s gyro horizon and was finally accepted for flight in this condition at midday.

'Wg Cdr Davies — Flight 3

He carried out stability tests at aft CG between 28% and 29% achieving this con-dition by suitable use of the tanks. Upon landing he stated that it was a most unusual experience to fly a prototype at Boscombe which was stable at its aft loading, and reported no marked tendency to diverge stick-free, and no tightening in the turn or loss of stick force per g. He remarked on the lack of major trim changes at 0.79M/20,000ft, and on the comparatively minor evidence of compressibility buffeting apparent there. He commented on the ability to fly for considerable periods stick- and rudder-free at high and low indicated speeds.

'After this flight the weather became unserviceable and a discussion was held with the B Squadron pilots on their early impressions.

'Wg Cdr Davies stated that he was beginning to feel that they would have only two major criticisms to offer; (1) that the canopy vision properties might be unacceptable and (2) that more tailplane travel was desirable to enable stick-free trimming wheels and flaps down at all loadings. While agreeing with (1) I pointed out that a high safety factor at altitude might well balance the scales against the vision disadvantage, and this was agreed to in principle. A compromise will, I am sure, be satisfactory in the case of (2).

'A subsequent discussion with Sqn Ldr Saxelby and Flt Lt Callard confirmed the above views and produced nothing further beyond the statement that "it is a very difficult aeroplane to criticise".

'On 1 November constant minor radio unserviceability delayed flying until after lunch.

'Sqn Ldr Saxelby — Flight 3

After handling at aft loading (27.5% to 29.05%) at 20,000ft he reported no instability at high or low speed, and remarked upon the ability to leave the aircraft at any high or low speed stick-free for long periods. He commented on directional stability and said "it does not snake at all".

'He criticised the inability to trim out the nose-up pitching moment wheels and flaps down at aft loading at any speed down to touchdown. He agreed that the aircraft is still reasonably controllable in spite of this and that the necessary push forces do not exceed reasonable limits. He reported excellent qualities at high IAS, and apparently exceeded the given limitations by reaching 460kts/0.75M/7,400ft. He did not find anything to criticise in the approach characteristics and had clearly become more accustomed to the type. He described the landing at aft CG as "no change in feel" and the aft loading characteristics at 20,000ft as "no apparent change in stick force per g from the normal case".

'The aircraft was serviceable at 10 o'clock on 2 November but weather prevented an early take-off.

'Flt Lt Callard — Flight 3

After handling at aft CG at 20,000ft he climbed to 40,000ft and reported considerable surprise at any lack of definite indication of the aft loading either at 20,000ft or at 40,000ft. He reported no deterioration of control or apparent loss of stick force per g, and stated that, "it handles at 40,000ft as it does at 20,000ft". He investigated the manoeuvre boundary and trim speed to 100kts at 40,000ft, and finally carried out a descent at maximum rate reaching 2,000ft in eight minutes from 40,000ft.

'Again he had nothing specific to criticise, but now stated that the machine does not snake, and commented very favourably on the lack of misting in the canopy. He commented that criticism of this machine is going to be extremely difficult, and he was quite clearly of the opinion that it is by far the best machine that has arrived at Boscombe for many years.

'Wg Cdr Davies — Flight 4

He climbed the machine to 45,000ft at aft loading and reported as follows:

'The machine handled easily at the highest altitude, but the falling off of power was noticeable above 40,000ft. There was no mist in the canopy and the cabin heat and pressurisation was excellent. The engine handling at altitude was simple and trouble-free, but he noted that the port throttle was considerably out of synchronisation with the starboard throttle above 35,000ft. He commented on engine vibrations at idling. He opened the bomb doors at 0.58M, 175kts, 40,000ft and stated that there was a slight buffet present but no trim change. He pulled $2\frac{1}{2}$g at 160kts at 35,000ft without buffet and only reached the buffeting point at $2\frac{3}{4}$g at this condition. He commented on the, "impressive ease of control throughout the flight range", with a special reference to the 44/45,000ft area.

'On 3 November there was no flying owing to minor unserviceability with personal radio equipment, and the day was occupied with final interrogation of the pilots and discussion of the future flying programme. This produced no further criticisms from the B Squadron pilots, but further superlatives and the assurance that, though at first they could not believe our claims for this machine, they now felt sure that the Canberra was an oustanding machine in every way, and that though they would be able to criticise minor details, they would have no far-reaching disagreement with our general opinion of the machine.

'Mr Wills stated that they intended to fly at the artificial full forward limit and (RPB) left them with the following suggestions, that:
1 the pilots should watch for neat elevator near touchdown at the full forward loading, and to trim the tail down slightly if required:
2 no full load single-engine flying should be done without prior firm's testing;
3 that the medium altitude temporary speed limit should be lowered to 0.74M above 4,000ft in order to guard against a recurrence of exceeding the limit laid down.

'Wg Cdr Davies and Mr Wills agreed to these points.

'Summary

After initial scepticism, the Canberra has proved its worth as a first-class flying machine, and the criticisms which have come to light to date are of only a minor nature.

'This rapid initial appraisal has been made possible by the excellent working of the Company's servicing party which has provided and continued to provide a high standard of daily serviceability. On many occasions the machine has been cleared for flight between 9 o'clock and 10 o'clock in the morning, and this has been done in spite of transport delays causing late arrivals in the morning, and of the complete absence of telephonic communications between the Canberra's dispersal and the remainder of the camp, two miles distant. A major factor in this increase in serviceability over normal conditions at Warton has clearly been the fact that, with clearance on a Form 700, engine runs and AID inspection have been completed after flying in the late afternoon, and the aircraft has been pushed out the following morning serviceable. The pilot has then signed for the aircraft and run the engines with AID inspection in the cockpit as a final check. It is recommended that this system, or something like it, be introduced on the Company's aerodromes if full advantage is to be taken of the short flying days of the winter.

'Continued serviceability has been in evidence since my departure on 4 October and two sorties a day were flown on Friday,

Saturday and Sunday. The general impression is that, given this continued serviceability, the preliminary trials will be complete by the end of the current week, and the machine will be ready for return to Warton on Friday 11 November.

R. P. Beamont
CHIEF TEST PILOT'

In the final outcome the trial was declared complete and successful on 14 November, and VN799 was returned to Warton.

A letter followed from the chief superintendent A&AEE, to Petter:

COPY

'Ministry of Supply,
     Aeroplane and Armament
     Experimental Establishment,
          Boscombe Down,
               Amesbury,
                    Wiltshire.
14th November, 1949

Dear Petter,
     The Canberra passed over my office just after 12 o'clock today on its way back to you after a very successful preliminary set of handling trials at Boscombe.

The report on the aeroplane is being prepared and should be available in the near future. I cannot wait to tell you, however, that the Squadron pilots have made a special point of emphasising the help given by Beamont in his discussions with them. He has apparently been very frank in telling them the doubtful points as well as the good points, and I don't think we found anything concerning the handling qualities of the aircraft that had not already been mentioned to us beforehand by your pilot. This happy state of affairs is very much appreciated and I hope it will continue in our future work on the Canberra and its successors.

We shall be ready to discuss our findings with you on Monday 28 November. Can you manage this date?

With kind regards,
Yours sincerely,
Ivor Bowen

W. E. W. Petter, Esq.,
     The English Electric Co. Ltd.,
          Aircraft Division,
               Warton Aerodrome,
                    Nr. Preston, Lancs.'

The second prototype, VN813 fitted with Nene engines, was flown from Warton on 9 November 1949 by Beamont who confirmed that as suspected the barrel-shaped engine nacelles resulted in a reduction of 0.05 in the Mach number handling limit to M0.8. Although not fully representative of 'production' aerodynamics VN813 proved useful for general Canberra engineering development flying until late 1950 when it was allotted to Rolls-Royce at Hucknall for Nene engine development work.

The third prototype, VN828, was a B Mk 1 built to a similar standard as VN799 and fitted with Avons. The first flight was on 22 November by Beamont, and it was the first Canberra flown from Samlesbury and landed at Warton, where it remained for the next five years on development flying.

The fourth and last B Mk 1 prototype, VN850 with Avon RA2 engines, was also similar to VN799 but with provision for jettisonable wing tip fuel tanks. The dorsal fillet forward of the fin on the earlier aircraft was removed on 850, and its rudder was built to the final rudder horn shape resulting from the handling trials on VN799.

With 850's first flight on 20 December 1949 by Beamont three prototypes had flown within a six-week period and all four in the eight months following 13 May.

During the summer of 1950 VN850 was used for clearance tests of the handling envelope with tip tanks, beginning on 11 May and ending with successful jettisoning of both tanks on 31 July. This test was carried out over Warton and the tanks were dropped with predicted accuracy into the triangle of grass subtended by the three runways at Warton with the Canberra on a southerly heading to ensure that in the event of an overshoot the tanks would fall over the Ribble marshes.

Top right:
The second prototype B1, VN813, with Nene engines in enlarged cowlings and the original dorsal fin. Seen here with the DH Spectre rocket installation at the 1956 Farnborough Display. *British Aerospace*

Centre right:
The third B1 prototype, VN828, on Warton tarmac in November 1949 with modified rudder, dorsal fin removed and the 'solid' radar nose. *British Aerospace*

Bottom right:
The fourth and last B1 prototype, VN850, before first flight at Warton in December 1949, with tip tanks fitted for handling and jettison trials and still retaining the original dorsal fin. *British Aerospace*

VN850 gave the first overseas Canberra display at Paris/Orly on 11 June taking only 54 minutes for the flight from Warton as a foretaste of its future record-breaking performances, and the acclaim rewarding its display at Orly was repeated at the Belgian international air show at Antwerp later in the month, where it was described as 'the star of the flying display' on 24 and 25 June.

On the flight back from Antwerp to Warton in 48min on 26 June, F. W. Page flew with Beamont for his first of many Canberra flights, and then on 30 June VN850 established another milestone in Canberra development by covering 1,600nm in three hours during an assessment of cruise-climb technique from 42,000 to 47,000ft.

Then followed an intensive period of display flying with VN850; first at Farnborough for the 1950 RAF Display from 4 to 10 July; then at Boscombe for demonstrations to a US mission; and finally Farnborough in September before it was delivered to Rolls-Royce for Avon engine development work at Hucknall from where it was eventually lost in a fatal accident at Bulwell Common on 13 June 1951.

Prior to this 850 became the first Canberra to reach 500kts IAS (50kts in excess of the required 'Service limit' of 450kts IAS) when completing position-error measurements past Blackpool Tower on 31 July.

Other milestones achieved by the prototypes during the first year were: with VN799 the first full load take off and nightflying on 16 October; first time to 45,000ft on 19 October; first time to 47,500ft on 21 October; and delivery for RAF preview trials to Boscombe Down on 28 October, Beamont with Joe Sarginson as passenger taking 19min for the 180nm flight.

50,000ft was reached by a Canberra for the first time with VN828 on 16 January 1950, and this flight exceeded the clearance limit of the partial-pressure-breathing system provided for the crew and resulted in a long and inconclusive debate with the authorities. The Ministry maintained that their 'approval' of tests was subject to observance of their limitations based on the equipment provided. English Electric flight operations took the view that the Canberra's potential needed to be proved before RAF service and that as the 47,000ft official clearance would not permit exploration of the full capability of the Canberra then they would accept responsibility; and by carrying on in this way increasing confidence was gained in the integrity of the pressure cabin, the cabin pressure system and the large one-piece 'blown' canopy.

Ultimately VX165, the prototype B Mk 2 in near-standard production configuration with RA3 engines of 6,500lb thrust, reached 54,500ft crewed by Beamont and Walker. This point with the rate of climb reduced to less than 100ft/min was regarded as the absolute ceiling and was not exceeded by any other production aircraft until the Lightning supersonic fighter and the Canberra PR9 also built by English Electric in the late 1960s.

8 Open Cockpit Canberra

The clearance testing of a major new type covers a wide range of activities ranging from repetitive data-gathering on stability, drag and performance through structural testing to handling and the establishment of acceptable control conditions throughout, and in some cases beyond, the normal design flight evelope boundaries of IAS, Mach number, altitude, normal acceleration and range.

Most of the testing is of a routine nature, but some of the extreme points can be more than interesting for the pilot! An example occurred with the B2 in 1951.

The one-piece 'blown' Perspex canopy had been shown to have good rain dispersal properties in causing even heavy rain to streak away without seriously impeding pilot vision, and in hundreds of hours of testing from 40,000ft to as high as 54,000ft its integrity on which the safety of the pressure cabin depended had not been faulted.

However the escape system included jettisoning of the whole canopy by explosive bolts and there was an official and not unreasonable requirement to demonstrate that control could be maintained in the event of loss of the canopy by accident or enemy fire; and this produced a different situation from aircraft with the more conventional strong windscreen structure which remains to protect the pilot when the canopy is ejected or lost.

Below:
Cockpit of 1st prototype VN799 showing the internal 'blast-protection' windscreen to protect the pilot in the event of loss of the jettisonable canopy. *IPC Press*

In the early Canberras all protection would be lost when the canopy went except for a minimal-sized flat glass panel directly in front of the pilot.

This was not liked by pilots as it reduced forward visibility by reflections, and wind tunnel tests had convinced the aerodynamics department that a much smaller deflector plate, over which the pilot could see without obstruction of vision, could be effective.

Accordingly a trials programme began with B2 WD935 on 12 April 1951 to establish the practical limits of flight without the canopy while retaining the small glass screen.

Beamont found that although draughty, it was possible to reach 400kts IAS, but that then the general buffeting became so heavy that there was likely to be damage to equip-ment and, possibly, loss of his goggles and mask which could make things difficult.

A second trial was carried out on 3 June 1951, this time with WD934 but with a metal deflector replacing the glass screen and about half its height.

This proved adequate protection up to over 400kts IAS (with the pilot's goggles lashed tight with tape), but vision over the nose was too restricted to be acceptable.

A final configuration was prepared and fitted to WD956 for trials which did not begin until 10 December 1951, uncomfortably on a day of hard frost. The new deflector plate was much reduced in size and Beamont, with face taped between mask and helmet as protection against frostbite, found that an absolute maximum of 445kts IAS could be tolerated, though with some discomfort.

This was accepted by the authorities as close enough to the Service limit speed of 450kts IAS, and the configuration went into production on the B2 and all subsequent variants of the basic B2 design.

Below:
B Mk 2 WD956 prepared for final testing with the canopy off on 10 December 1951. The ejector seat has been heavily taped to protect the mechanism as has the pilot's face against frostbite. *British Aerospace*

9 The Canberra B Mk 2

Canberra B Mk 2 Official Description (Specification B5/47)

Description

This aircraft is a midwing monoplane and powered by engines mounted in the wings, carrying a crew of 3 who are provided with a means for ejection. The fuselage is a stressed skin of semi-monocoque construction, the nose portion being pressurised with hot/cold control. The upper centre fuselage holds fuel tanks 1, 2 and 3,. the lower part being the bomb compartment, enclosed by hydraulically retractable doors. The tail portion is of a standard pattern with variable incidence tailplane. Provision is made for a 300gal LR tank in the bomb bay and jettisonable tanks are carried on the wing tips. Refuelling of all tanks is by ordinary ground methods, through large orifices.

Engines

Number: Two Rolls-Royce jet propelled engines
Type: Avon Mk 1/RA3
Dry Weight: 2,276lb
Engine Rating: Thrust 6,500lb each engine
Starting: Rolls-Royce turbostarter by cartridge

Operational Equipment

VHF   (ARI 5490)
Gee H   (ARI 5829)
Rebecca   (ARI 5610)
Orange Putter   (ARI 5800)
Radio Altimeter AYF   (ARI 5284)
Radio Compass, Marconi   AD 7092D
IFF Mk 10   (ARI 5848)
Blue Shadow can be fitted to S00

Dimensions

Span: 64ft   *Length:* 65ft 6in
Height: 15ft 7in
Sweep back at $\frac{1}{4}c$: 13° 33'
Wing thickness   12% at root
cord: 9% at tip
Track: 15ft 9in at main wheels
Wheelbase: (triangular) 14ft forward of main wheels

Armament

1×5,000lb HC or 2×4,000lb HC or 6×1,000lb bombs
With roles for the above 1×F24 camera or low level night photographic role 2×F97 Mk 2 cameras and photoflashes, or Target role — 300gal bomb bay tank with 3×1,000lb target bombs, or Window launcher
Total fuselage fuel weight=10,992lb
Maximum bomb load=10,000lb. With this load acceleration is slightly reduced

Fuel

Centre Fuselage Tanks:
No 1 tank   512gal
No 2 tank   317gal
No 3 tank   545gal
Wing tip
Jettisonable tanks, 2 tanks,
250gal each   500gal

Total: 1,874gal

Controls

Flaps: Split type   *Total area:* 73sq ft
Dive brakes: Type: Finger spoiler, drag channel section. Hydraulically operated
Area: (inner face of brakes to air stream only) 596.8sq in
Manually operated controls: Electrically operated for trimming purposes only and electrically operated tailplane

Note: Spring tabs are fitted to control surfaces

Fuel Avtag or Kerosine
Engine *oil* capacity — 17pt each (300gal fuel tank can be fitted in bomb bay if required)

Two prototypes were built to this specification with revised cockpit accommodation for three crew members including an ejection seat for the bomb-aimer alongside the navigator's position, and a forward prone position for bomb-aiming in a new glazed nose section accommodating a T2 optical bombsight.

The first prototype, VX165, flew on 23 April 1950 and the second, VX169, on 2 August 1950, both powered by Avon 101 (RA3 series) engines with 6,500lb st; and these were followed by the first production aircraft, WD929, on 8 October 1950 at Samlesbury.

165 and 169 completed intensive handling and engineering assessments at Warton during the remainder of 1950 and early 1951, and these were successful in achieving clearance into service (CA Release) by the spring of 1951 when production B2 WD936 was the first Canberra delivered for squadron service — to No 101 Squadron, Binbrook on 25 May 1951.

Entry into service was reasonably trouble free with the RAF understandably showing considerable caution at the quantum jump in performance of the Canberra in comparison with the Lincoln which it replaced; but soon the tempo changed.

Impressed with the ease of maintenance and operation of their new charge and inspired by their commander, Sir Dermot Boyle, No 2 Group announced plans for an ambitious Canberra tour of South America. The story of this successful operation is covered elsewhere in this book, but there were many who felt that to set off across the world with minimal engineering support at so early a stage in the life of this new aircraft was courting disaster.

Nevertheless the outcome was resounding success and the only major technical problem encountered during the South American tour was recurrent unserviceability of their support Hastings aircraft!

Soon after the successful South American tour a serious technical defect became apparent resulting in some fatal accidents, the first of which were unexplained. Then reports began to come in of apparent 'runaway' failures of the tailplane electrical trimmer actuation, and immediate intensive trials were carried out at Warton to re-establish the limits of controllability available to the pilot in the event of a tailplane running away to full travel in either direction.

With anticipation from knowledge that a 'failure' was about to happen and in otherwise favourable conditions, the pilot could 'hold' a nosedown or noseup 'runaway' safely up to about 350kts IAS, but above this control deteriorated rapidly and at speeds above 400kts the situation was uncontrollable.

The Warton test pilots flew again and again into conditions which would normally be considered unacceptable with the aircraft diving out of control despite a full strength two-handed pull on the control yoke, and one final incident convinced everyone that enough was enough.

In production B Mk 2 WH715 Desmond (Dizzy) de Villiers had been briefed to action a full nosedown 'runaway' at forward cg at 420kts IAS/10,000ft, and as expected the Canberra plunged down against full 'up' elevator while de Villiers quickly pulled back the throttles and opened the airbrakes. However as his left hand came off the yoke to reach the throttles the dive steepened and this time both engines flamed out under the sustained negative g.

Giving a May Day call de Villiers said he was below 7,000ft but pulling out of the dive and starting engine relight drills.

Then, in his next call 'At 2,000ft descending. Both relights failed. Am over the sea in thick haze. Will bale out if final relighting attempt fails'. There was nothing more from his radio, and full emergency action was started until about an hour later he telephoned to say that he had landed on the deserted wartime airfield at Millom, by then an army training area, which had appeared out of the mist just as he was preparing to eject. He had lowered the undercarriage and landed on the 'nearest runway' still without engine power, and after a rough ride down the old airfield suface had stopped amid 'piles of rubble' and surrounded by soldiers who seemed highly suspicious of his motives for landing unannounced on, 'their training ground'!

A ground party from Warton found that there was only minor damage and after they had serviced the engine starting and relighting system, de Villiers flew it back to Warton the next day.

It was before this period that Preston's first fatal Canberra accident occurred. WD991, a production aircraft on test from Samlesbury on 25 March 1952, crashed soon after take-off at Lea, west of Preston, and test pilot Tommy Evans was killed.

The aircraft had gone in to a steep dive, and in the virtually complete destruction there were no relevant technical clues.

The time and distance from take-off were consistent with the first high-speed trim point in the test schedule and this suggested that a runaway tailplane was one of the possibilities; but there was no evidence to prove this or any other cause.

Meantime, with tailplane runaway incidents mounting there was an upsurge of concern in the RAF. The results of the flight tests and comprehensive technical reviews were soon in hand and English Electric represented by Page, Crowe, Beamont and electrical design specialist Cliff Tarr from Warton, attended a priority meeting with RAF and RAE specialists at Farnborough, chaired by the Director of the RAE.

At this a powerful attack was made by the RAF team led by an air marshal, on the integrity of the English Electric Co and of their design, engineering and flight test staff for what was described as a negligent approach to the design and clearance of an unsafe system which could, 'run away and become uncontrollable'.

By this time the cause of the failures had been positively traced to mechanical, 'sticking-on' of the single-pole trim switch which had caused the actuator to run on to full travel after the pilot had released the switch.

The RAF claimed that this was gross negligence by the design organisation, and that as more lives would be lost if a solution were not found they would recommend grounding the fleet. They had a good point but were wide of their aiming mark in apportioning blame, for the mechanical and electrical design of the tailplane trim system had been investigated, approved and authorised by many tiers of officials in the formal procurement and official approval system of the Ministry of Supply; so that if blame had to be laid anywhere it was palpably a collective one.

Page countered this blast with a statement of the company's further test experiences and proposals for improvements in the electrical and mechanical design, and recommended that there should be no grounding, but temporary limitations to a relatively low speed at which the pilot could hold any runaway, as demonstrated at Warton.

This was accepted by the Director RAE, though under a note of protest by the RAF, and in a maximum effort all marks of Canberra were progressively refitted with a modification scheme which included a new

Right:
Esme Watson, Pat Beamont, Tommy Evans and Peter Hillwood watch WD940 leaving Warton for the USA, 31 August 1951.
British Aerospace

duplicated (dipole) trim switch, improvements in wiring integrity and revised actuator stops reducing the overall travel. These measures eliminated the problem, but it was some time before the previous high level of confidence was restored in the RAF at user level who, advised by their seniors, continued to see English Electric as solely to blame for what was in fact the joint responsibility of a number of involved authorities. In aircraft design it is easy to be wise after the event, and seldom possible to get everything right first time.

As with all new aircraft the Canberra encountered some technical problems during development and in its Service life, but they were relatively few and all were overcome in time.

The most difficult short-term fault was the runaway trimming tailplane problem, and sadly a number of lives were lost before it was put right.

Another defect which gave much trouble during development and early production flight testing became known as 'freezing ailerons' but was in fact due to varying production tolerances in the clearance between the aileron 'beaks' and shrouds. The effect of this was that in a fast climb on a cold day at altitude, the aileron 'beak' would progressively pick up on a high point on the shroud, and the pilot would become conscious of heavying aileron hinge moment and reduction in rolling power.

Then, if he continued to climb, aileron forces would increase to a point where the wheel could be moved only in jerks and lateral control would disappear leaving a 'crossed aileron' response as the torque tube wound on tab against the jammed aileron.

This was a peculiar effect and rather disturbing for the pilot until, during the subsequent emergency descent, control was felt to come back gradually as height was lost. This gave the clue that differential expansion and contraction was causing an interference foul at some high point, and on opening up the shrouds on the ground, score marks on the paint finish confirmed the point-source of the trouble.

Another serious and more long-term problem was stress corrosion resulting from the use of the specified 'new' material DTD 683, an aluminium alloy containing zinc which was confidently thought to be the best material available for the anticipated high levels of stress associated with 'jet' speeds. This confidence proved to be unfounded and difficulty was experienced with early production aircraft until these materials were changed in later production to DTD 5094.

This gave rise to some major work in later years when the first batch aircraft returned for overhaul, and in some cases the centre spar forgings themselves had to be replaced.

In the first B Mk 2 production batches undercarriage sequence-valve defects caused losses of 'D' doors during flight testing, and some delays in clearing aircraft.

Another problem area which resulted in a change to the production test schedule was the appearance of variations in longitudinal trimming to, in some cases, beyond the acceptable limits of the tailplane actuator.

This resulted in a revised schedule of tests and adjustments which remained an essential part of the production flight test schedule for the next 30 years.

But after these had been resolved the flight development and subsequent production testing of all variants of the Canberra were straightforward, lacking in severe complication and generally described by those involved as 'no bother at all'.

Series Production

The Mk 2 was the definitive production aircraft on which the initial RAF and early export orders were based.

Built in greater quantity than any of the later variants, many B2s survived over 30 years to serve in a multitude of operational and general support roles into the 1980s, with a strong possibility that some would still be flying in the year 2000.

The main UK production contracts were placed not with English Electric alone but also with Handley Page, Avro and Short and Harland, on the basis apparently that Preston were not thought to have the capacity to reach the required production rate.

With the passage of time it seems more probable that the split was made in order to safeguard production capacity at the subcontractors until their own V-bomber contenders could reach production, and to solve for a time part of the perennial problem of continuity of employment in Northern Ireland; but there can be no reasonable doubt that the production expertise of English Electric, Preston, could have controlled an expanded programme, based on the subcontracting of some components where necessary, which could have met the requirement at significantly less cost to the taxpayer than that of setting up three new production lines in various parts of the country. But that is not always the way of government departments.

10 The Flight Development Period

The period from 1949 to 1954 was one of massive test activity at Warton, firstly to prove the handling and performance of this new military jet, then to develop modifications where necessary, and finally to establish the performance of the varied equipments associated with the different marks, beginning with the bombing and reconnaissance systems, then the low-level strike systems for the B(I)6 and B(I)8, and finally the tactical nuclear delivery system for the B(I)8.

The longest serving development aircraft was WD937. This was one of the first production batch B2s which originally came to Warton from Samlesbury for investigation after failing to pass its production test schedule owing to excessive vibration.

It stayed on as a general test vehicle for trial installations and became a long-term trial aircraft for the power-controlled rudder which was eventually introduced to the PR9.

Although noted for docility and ease of control, all Canberra marks suffered from one controversial shortcoming — with twin, powerful engines relatively widely spaced apart, single-engine controllability could be a problem and although Warton flight operations had been able to recommend safety speeds which would cover most operational circumstances, they could not cover engine failure in a critical area in full-load take-off, or in final approach conditions at very low speed.

These aspects were regarded as an acceptable risk as with other aircraft in service, but after some accidents in the early 1950s involving single-engine recovery it became apparent that some confident operators were using lower than the recommended safety speeds.

Right, top to bottom:
WD937 belly-lands on a foam path at Warton with undercarriage failure, but pilot Keith Isherwood walks away unharmed. *British Aerospace*

48

Warton reiterated their warning that 145kts was the safe low-load minimum single-engine speed and correspondingly higher speeds at higher weights, and during the trials on WD937 it became clear that the power rudder could lower the range of critical speeds by at least 25kts overall. There was a very clear case on safety grounds for retrospectively modifying the fleet but although this was proposed formally on a number of occasions it was rejected on economic grounds until the advent of the PR9 which, with its much more powerful engines, demanded the power rudder system even to maintain the safety speeds of the earlier marks, and then only with use of less than maximum power for take-off.

Statistically the Canberra had a better-than-average accident rate throughout its long in-service life in the RAF, but with the power rudder it could have been even safer.

WD937 remained at Warton until 1968 performing a wide range of duties from trial installations of new equipments and performance testing, to photographic and 'chase' sorties with new developments of Lightnings, overseas Canberras, Strikemasters, Jaguars and ultimately the prototype TSR2.

For the latter programme 937 was civil-registered G-ATZW in all-black finish, having been bought in by the company when it was declared surplus to requirements by the Ministry.

During its 16 years of valuable and reliable service at Warton it had recorded only one serious incident. In 1966 while flown by production test pilot Keith Isherwood the undercarriage failed to lower, and after prolonging the flight to burn off fuel while Warton fire brigade crash crews prepared a foam path to reduce friction damage and the risk of fire, Isherwood brought it in for a smooth belly landing. Damage was so slight that 937 was flying again in less than a week, and the cause of the undercarriage malfunction was found to be a servicing error.

Above:
WD937 in civil livery as Warton's private chase/support aircraft, 1964-67.
British Aerospace

Left:
Three great all-British aircraft: Canberra WD937, still at Warton in 1965; and the two supersonic aircraft it had flown with as chase aircraft — the prototype TSR2 and a Lightning Mk 6.
British Aerospace

11 Canberra for America

In August 1950 a message was received at Warton Flight Operations that an important demonstration was required of the Canberra for some American VIPs. It was to take place at RAF Burtonwood and Warton was asked to comment on the practicability of this.

This was at a time of total concentration on the urgent test programme with its target of entry into RAF service by spring 1951, and so Warton responded in a memorandum stating that Burtonwood was suitable for a demonstration but that due to test programme pressures it was not proposed to send a support ground party, and the pilot would land, take off and demonstrate and then fly back to Warton, all without stopping engines.

Surprisingly enough this was accepted by the Directors and the Ministry authorities, and it was subsequently learnt that although serious interest was being shown in the Canberra by the USAF, with true British reserve those responsible on this side regarded the Canberra as 'promising but unproved' and the whole idea of possible sales to America as premature and a little ridiculous.

Nevertheless it seemed that the Americans were determined and after further test flights on the morning of 17 August Beamont flew B Mk 2 aircraft VX169 the short hop to Burtonwood in poor weather conditions of drizzle and leaden grey sky with a lowering cloud base which, as he peered at it through the rain-streaked canopy, looked like inhibiting the demonstration.

However as the wide expanse of the USAF maintenance base appeared rain-glistening out of the murk about three miles ahead, the main cloud base was around 3,000ft and RPB decided to keep in the looping plane manoeuvres he had planned; it being one of the features that intrigued the aviation world at the time and subsequently that this new jet bomber was able to show even more manoeuvrability than the current crop of jet fighter prototypes.

With no traffic on this almost deserted postwar airfield VX169 was landed after a close circuit to assess the demonstration area and 'display line' given by Air Traffic, and then taxied in towards the small group of raincoat-clad people with staff cars. Flight Test engineer Dave Walker went forward and opened the hatch letting in the roar of the engines, and one by one the group of earnest civilians and uniformed USAF generals peered into the cockpit.

After a long walk-round inspection by the VIPs, Air Cdre Strang Graham, the English Electric Co aircraft sales manager, gave a thumbs-up signal for the demonstration to begin.

It had now stopped raining and with full power and very light loading with less than 3,000lb fuel the Canberra was airborne in under 700yd, and then pulled up steeply into its characteristic 'cartwheel' wing-over to come back down the runway and pull up at 370kts into a roll-off and begin a display uninhibited by traffic or other restrictions.

Some minutes later with the fuel gauges showing a distinct need for an early landing, VX169 gave the attentive group on the tarmac a final low pass and headed north for Warton.

Soon after this, in September, a team of USAF test pilots and engineers headed by Col Al Boyd, chief of the USAF test centre at Wright Field, Ohio, came to Warton and after an intensive flying programme guardedly pronounced themselves impressed with the Canberra.

Getting back at once to the test programme the Warton team had almost forgotten all this when, in January 1951, information came in to the effect that despite actual advice by the government that the Canberra was in too early a stage of its development, the Americans were insisting on a full evaluation in competition with their currently emerging jet bomber prototypes. These were the Martin XB-51 and North American B-45, the propeller-driven North American AJ-1 and Douglas A-26, and also the Canadian Avro CF-100; and the competition was for an aircraft to meet a USAF requirement for a

medium-range 'Intruder'. Staff work was apparently well advanced, but the Pentagon were demanding a 'fly-off' comparison before a formal decision could be made.

Accordingly the RAF had agreed to release one of their 'pre-production' Canberra trial aircraft WD932 and to deliver it to Washington in February.

Soon after this news was received at Warton, Beamont was told to go to Washington to fly the Canberra in the competition, and to introduce it subsequently at the Middle River factory of the Glenn L. Martin Company which had been chosen to build Canberras under licence if it were selected.

Sqn Ldr Arthur Callard with his navigator Flt Lt Haskett and signaller Flt Lt Robson safely delivered WD932 to Andrews Air Force Base Washington on 21 February 1951 after completing the first direct jet crossing of the Atlantic in record-breaking time and taking 4hr 37min for the 1,800nm from Aldergrove to Gander.

The aircraft arrived fit and fully serviceable, and with Warton's Flight Shed Superintendent Bill Eaves and an English Electric servicing team, Beamont took WD932 over at Andrews on the following day.

The briefing for the comparative display for the Senior Officers' Board of the Pentagon on 26 February 1951, at which Beamont was the only foreigner present, all the other pilots being Air Force or American company test

Top:
WD932's crew meet the Martin Co Management, February 1951. Left to right: Chet Pearson, Glen L. Martin, Sqn Ldr Arthur Callard, and Flt Lts Haskett and Robson, RAF. *Martin Co*

Above:
Canberra on foreign ground — Baltimore USA, February 1951. *Martin Co*

Right:
Control tower and flight test at Martin, Middle River. *Martin Co*

pilots, was conducted by a USAF major in the presence of the colonel commanding the base and was strictly formal and 'by the book'.

Beamont was initially concerned when hearing that each aircraft was to fly the same set pattern of simple manoeuvres in a 10-minute time 'slot', and he eventually asked if the patterns could be varied to suit particular aircraft. 'No', he was told firmly. 'This is an Air Force trial and not a Farnborow show!'

But then he realised that the Canberra could complete the set manoeuvres in about half the set time — and no-one had said anything about what to do with any time saved, so he resolved not to waste it.

On the 26th the weather was crisp and clear with a high overcast. The programme on the Operation Room board showed the B-45 first off and the Canberra taking off last after the XB-51.

Predictably the American aircraft flew their routines safely, but unimpressively owing mainly to universally high wing loadings and moderate power-to-weight ratios. Even the A-26 and AJ-1, though relatively manoeuvrable aircraft, could not perform to advantage within the set turns and fly-bys.

Only the XB-51 looked a new and impressive shape on its rather infrequent fly-bys, but its very high wing loading and low manoeuvre capability obviously limited is presentation severely. Then its time was up and it was the turn of the last item on the programme.

Making full use of the controllability of the Canberra and of its low wing loading WD932 was flown through all the set manoeuvres within the boundary of the big military airfield, and when completing a final tight

Left:
932 demonstrates at Baltimore, March 1956; this aircraft was lost over Chesapeake Bay in December 1951. *Martin Co*

Below:
Chet Pearson, Pat Tibbs (Martin Chief Test Pilot), RPB. *Martin Co*

turn on to the approach with gear and flaps down it had 4½ minutes to go until the end of the 10-minute slot. So raising the gear and flaps and opening up the fast-accelerating RA3 Avon engines to full power, the Canberra zoom-climbed over the heads of the spectators, pulled into a minimum-radius 360° turn directly overhead, half-rolled down into a 400kts flypast and back up into a 'cartwheel' wing-over followed by a power-off-and-airbrakes tight spiral dive to pull out in front of the spectators, and then up and over again into the downwind pattern, whistling almost silently with power off and bringing in throttle only to adjust the approach speed after lowering gear and flaps again in a tight left bank prior to landing.

At this point when braking to a standstill Beamont felt both mainwheels lock and tyres burst. He had failed to notice (and had not been briefed) that the white concrete runway had only recently been heavily sanded for ice; this sand was invisible and it naturally produced a highly abrasive surface unsuited to heavy braking. A voice from the navigator's seat of the USAF evaluation team officer carried as 'observer' said, 'Gee, that's more manoeuvrability than I've ever seen'; and no-one at Andrews seemed bothered by the tyrebursts at all as there was no other damage, and the controllability of the landing run had obviously not been seriously affected.

As described in the definitive account of the Canberra in USAF service, *B-57 Canberra at War* (Bob Mikesh, Ian Allan Ltd 1980) the decision to select the Canberra may possibly have been taken prior to the Andrews 'fly-off', but there can be little doubt that had the Canberra failed on that day a USAF Canberra pro-

gramme would never have materialised in the face of a revitalised anti-foreign purchase lobby which came very close to prevailing as it was.

But now the Canberra was on its way to equipping the United States Air Force in which it still served 30 years later.

USAF production and service

The United States' decision to acquire the Canberra as its main night-intruder aircraft was promulgated on 23 March 1951, in a letter to the Martin Company authorising the manufacture of 250 B-57As. A licence agreement was concluded between Martin and English Electric on 3 April that year. Royalties were fixed at not more than five per cent of a fair selling price of the aircraft.

Martin signed up major sub-contractors to produce B-57 parts, including Kaiser Metals (wing panels, nacelles, bomb bay doors), Hudson Motors (rear fuselage and tail) and Cleveland Pneumatic Tool Co (landing gears). Manufacturing rights to produce the Armstrong Siddeley J65 Sapphire engine cost the Wright Aeronautical Corporation $499,800, and manufacture was sub-contracted to Buick, a division of General Motors. The Sapphire developed 7,200lb thrust compared with the 6,500lb of the Rolls-Royce Avon RA3 in the British Canberras, a necessary increment in view of extra weight which the Americans proposed to put into the B-57.

Two DC-4 loads of Canberra drawings on loft plates arrived from English Electric at the beginning of June 1951, and the massive job of converting them to US measurement and tolerance standards was begun at once by the Martin Company, which was impressed by EE's speed of reaction. Meanwhile, flight trials with a Canberra 'on bail' from the RAF to the USAF went on. This was B2 WD932, and in August 1951 it was joined by a second bailed B2, WD940, which on its delivery flight set up an official record from Aldergrove, Northern Ireland, to Gander, of 4hr 18min at an average speed of 481.1mph over the 2,072 statute-mile route. WD940 joined WD932 at Martin's on 4 September and took part in trials designed to produce a flow of development information between the USAF and the RAF.

During the second USA delivery flight (of WD940 on its second stage from Gander to Martin Middle River near Baltimore) considerable interest was shown by the air traffic and radar reporting centres, and from Bangor, Maine came a direct request for the Canberra's altitude. RPB replied that that was, 'classified information' but that he was, 'well above any airways traffic'.

This did not satisfy the military ATC, and a little later when approaching Cape Cod which could be seen in clear morning sunshine over 100 miles ahead, New York metropolitan area control demanded height information insistently. RPB again politely refused, sensing that a defence exercise was in operation which was soon confirmed by the presence of criss-crossing fighter vapour trials far below. He checked the fuel state and dis-

Left:

A DC-4 load of Canberra design data about to leave Warton for America. In front are the USAF engineers, with EE personnel (left to right: Strang Graham, Page, Crowe, Hollock, Howatt, Ellis, Ellison, Hothersal, D. Smith) in May 1951. *British Aerospace*

Above:

Key people at Middle River in 1951; left to right: Glen Hobday, R. Beamont, George Cook (Martin Co), F. W. Page. *Martin Co*

tance to run with Watson and then opened up to climb power to take the Canberra to 50,000ft as they passed overhead New York. The F-86 Sabres below would have a hard time trying to intercept from their maximum operating height of about 42,000ft.

On arrival at Middle River, Beamont was told that a meeting had been arranged for the following day at the Pentagon and that it would be with the Senior Officers' Board of the USAF. At this meeting, which RPB recalls was in a small room almost totally filled with heavily-beribboned generals, there was some formal discussion about the capabilities of the Canberra and on its behaviour in long-distance flights, and then when it began to seem that no major points would arise came

the question: 'There seemed to be some communications problem yesterday — what height were you over Long Island?'

RPB said '50,000ft' and explained the British radio security requirement. This caused a buzz of interest and amazement and when the whistles and gee-wizzes died down one voice said, 'but still, ATC require height information for safety separation'. 'Certainly', said RPB, 'but there weren't going to be any other aircraft up there, were there!'

By the end of the summer of 1951 it was apparent that the Canberra's debut in the USA had been a major success on all counts and the programme to manufacture it as the B-57 for the USAF got swiftly into its stride at Martin's Middle River plant.

WD932, still in its RAF insignia, was used in 'stage 2' official trials by the USAF to make heavy-weight take-offs at 48,000lb to simulate the weight of the B-57A, but on 21 December 1951, the aircraft crashed in Maryland when a wing failed as the pilot was pulling a 4.8G test point at 10,000ft. The USAF pilot and observer ejected, but the latter's parachute failed to open and he was killed.

Subsequent test flights by Beamont in WD958 with careful CG control repeating the manoeuvres which had preceded disaster to WD932, proved conclusively that the structure was safe and that was no basic design fault. What had happened to 932, it was determined, was that incorrect scheduling of fuel usage had resulted in the balance of the aircraft becoming tail-heavy, so that on entering the tight turn the machine had become longitudinally unstable and pitched up overstressing the wings and producing a failure of the left wing near to the engine nacelle.

The accident brought into the open feelings which had been building up at the Wright Air Development Center that the Canberra should be extensively modified before it went into USAF service — feelings which had been damped down up to that point by the insistence by the USAF that, on cost grounds, the Canberra should pass virtually unmodified from the RAF to the USAF. Maj-Gen F. R. Dent, CO of WADC, listed what he considered to be 31 deficiencies in a letter to his headquarters, and backed up his case by enclosing a letter from the Ministry of Supply in London to English Electric. This also listed items which the Ministry was demanding should be put right before the aircraft went to the RAF, and Dent noted that the two lists were very similar.

Air Material Command accepted the modification case, and even though production was already in full swing at Martin on the 'A' model, modifications of this original B-57 design were ordered — resulting in the B-57B. The most noticeable change was a new tandem cockpit arrangement which gave better visibility in ground attack operations, enabled the navigator to be moved from the original compartment inside the fuselage to a place where he could see out clearly (and had a better chance of getting out in case of emergency), and replaced the all-curved canopy with one which was much longer and which had a flat glass panel in a conventional windscreen structure at the front. It had been found that it was impossible to put a gunsight behind the curved canopy and have it harmonise accurately with the guns because the canopy flexed with changes of pressure and temperature, especially when the aircraft was flying fast and low.

Other important modifications included speed brakes positioned at the aircraft's waist, a starter system on the J65 engine which employed a cartridge which when fired produced a pall of black smoke (and premature action from many *ab initio* station firemen), and a rotating bomb bay door. Designed by two Martin engineers this piece of equipment was 17ft long and, mounted in two pivots, could open in four seconds and shut in six. Bombs were attached to the inside of the door, which could be opened without producing buffeting — and therefore, without speed restrictions in the target area. This device made the B-57 suitable as a vehicle for LABS Low Altitude Bombing System), or low-level delivery of theatre nuclear weapons. The procedure that was practised was for the aircraft to approach the target fast and very low, then pull up sharply in a half-loop so 'tossing' the weapon up to 9,000ft, while rolling out into a speedy getaway in the reverse direction.

The B-57s also added sophisticated (for that time) bombing aids, a radar detection system which warned of other aircraft and eight underwing hard points for rockets and bombs. In later models off the production line, four 20mm M-39 cannon with 290 rounds each were carried in the wings and replaced the eight .50 calibre machine guns of the 'A' model.

Back at English Electric it was considered that many of these changes incorporated an element of political 'window dressing' although the cockpit and bomb bay were clear improvements for the USAF roles. It was noted that no other major structural or safety design changes were made and that the main alterations were all to meet the new requirements of the USAF. Later, Beamont flight-tested both the B-57A and B-57B and found their performance virtually indistinguishable from the comparable UK versions, the B Mk 2 and the B(I)8.

Eight aircraft were completed by Martin as B-57As with some modifications incorporated, and they became standard as the reconnaissance version. Throughout the entire redesign phase, EE was represented at Martin's by Glen Hobday, who was acknowledged by both companies to have made a major contribution to the success of this complicated international collaboration project.

The first B-57A made its maiden flight on 20 July 1953, two years and four months after Martin had been given the contract. One month later, on 20 August, the aircraft was formally handed over to the USAF. But although this was a remarkably short time, the development path did not run smoothly. Kaiser had trouble in meeting the timetable for the production of wing panels with the result that the work was taken over by Martin; while the first J65 engines from Buick did not come up to specification, mainly because of problems of converting to US standards. Wright Aeronautical Corp eventually took on engine production.

Inevitably, as the result of such a rushed programme, there were development problems with both airframe and engine, including a number of fatal accidents resulting in aircraft groundings while corrective action was taken. But this is not to gainsay the tremendous achievement of Martin and its sub-contractors who, between them, produced a total of 403 B-57s in six different versions within three and a half years. Throughout its life in the USAF it was generally known as the B-57, although in the original letter of agreement signed by English Electric and Martin, one paragraph read: 'Martin shall name all aircraft manufactured by it under this agreement 'Canberra' in accordance with the usual practice of Martin with respect to other aircraft of its manufacture, and shall use its best efforts to procure the agreement of the Government of the United States of America that the same name shall be used by the Government of the United States of America.'

The 363rd Tactical Reconnaissance Wing of the USAF was the first unit to take the B-57 on to its strength, receiving 'A' versions in

Left:
WD932 flies over Baltimore in USAF markings.
British Aerospace via D. Woods

Below:
The first Martin B-57 A model over Chesapeake Bay in 1953.
Martin Co

Above:
The first production batch of B-57A models, for reconnaissance, in 1954. *Martin Co*

1954. First to receive the 'B' bomber version was the 345th Bomb Group (Tactical), which had previously flown 'As' to get to know their new charges. By 1957, four tactical bomber groups were equipped, including one in France, and one in the Far East. Training was carried out in Texas at Randolph Air Force Base, which had some of the first 'Bs' and 'C' dual-control trainer versions assigned to it.

By 1959, three of the four groups had been disbanded, including the 38th which, from its base at Laon, France, had become renowned for its Black Knights — believed to have been the world's first aerobatic team to feature bombers rather than fighters. The last group, the 3rd Bomb Wing, based in Japan but rotated through Kunsan, Korea, where its nuclear weapons were stored, was about to be stood down and its B-57s ferried home to the National Guard when the growing fighting in Vietnam changed all the plans.

Two B-57 squadrons were deployed from the Philippines where they had been held in readiness, to Bien Hoa air base near Saigon soon after the Gulf of Tonkin incident in early August 1964, when a US destroyer was attacked by North Vietnamese torpedo boats. The squadrons sat at Bien Hoa for seven months, carrying out reconnaissance duties before becoming involved in the fighting. Five out of 20 B-57s parked on the base were destroyed during a nighttime mortar attack by the Viet Cong during November that year.

B-57s went into action on 19 February 1965, when a total of 18 attacked a reported concentration of Viet Cong to the east of Saigon. All returned to base safely.

Above left:
The B-57B model with new nose fuselage, 1 April 1956.
USAF photo

Left:
A B model in flight showing the tandem crew arrangement.
Martin Co

Below:
Three B-57Bs in night black intruder finish. *USAF photo*

Reinforced from Clark Air Base in the Philippines, the B-57s were soon mounting regular attacks. One such on a military staging area 17 miles north of the demilitarised zone, is graphically described in his excellent book *Canberra B-57 At War* by Robert C. Mikesh who flew the type extensively with the USAF.

'Despite one day delay due to weather, the attackers became airborne at 14.50hrs on 2 March, dampened only by a drizzling rain. One aircraft aborted out of 20, and it was replaced by one of two airborne spares. The Canberra crews were leaving nothing to chance for not giving a good showing. Spaced ten minutes apart, the bomber formations of five flights of four planes each passed their checkpoint at Da Nang. Here they turned their radios to the target area control frequency, only to be stunned to hear that three F-105 flak-suppression aircraft had already been downed by intense AA fire in the target area. Heavy resistance was expected, and this confirmed it.

'The bombers pressed on and as the former capital city of Hue came in sight, they went "on the deck" to avoid radar detection until the pop-up for the actual dive bomb run. All crews were to make one pass only, releasing all ordnance, but a second pass could be made only if the first was not successful. At the time of the arrival of the lead flight on the target, parts of the target were already smoking from flak suppression ordnance. The Canberras, led by Major Roy White, came in and dropped without difficulty.

'Some battle damage was incurred, but none serious enough to cause any major problems. The Canberra crews felt they had at last earned their place when bomb damage assessment photos showed over 95% destruction in the target area. The heavy loads carried by the B-57s had indeed proven most deadly against the North Vietnamese. The 20 aircraft dropped over 96 tons of bombs, with a distance to the target of 450 miles.'

The USAF lost its first B-57 in action on 11 March 1965, when an aircraft burst into flames during an attack and crashed beyond the target area. During the same month, B-57s began training for the main purpose for which they were taken into the inventory — night interdiction. One of their main tasks was to attack traffic moving under cover of darkness down the Ho Chi Minh trail, and the usual procedure was to rendezvous in pairs with a C-130 Hercules which would drop flares to illuminate the road below, giving the B-57s the opportunity to carry out strafing runs.

B-57s stayed in Vietnam until October 1969, bearing much of the bombing brunt of that conflict and gaining the reputation with the USAF as the best night interdiction aircraft of the war. They also proved that the basic Canberra design was capable of speedy turnround under active service conditions, and of soaking up a great deal of punishment from enemy action. A number returned from missions with large sections of their airframe either riddled or missing, but thanks to the

simple basic design and the skill and dedication of the USAF ground crews who frequently 'cannibalised' other B-57s for spares, their availability for action was always high.

According to Mikesh, of 96 B-57s assigned to two bomb squadrons in South-East Asia, only one out of every three survived the war. One sensational loss occurred early on when, at Bien Hoa air base in May 1965, a B-57 loaded with 13 bombs blew up as its crew was about to start engines before taking off on a raid. As a result of the explosion, 10 B-57s,

11 Vietnamese Air Force A-1Hs and a USN F-8 Crusader were destroyed, 28 officers and men were killed, and a further 105 wounded.

To make up for the losses of B-57s in Vietnam, Martin converted, in late 1965, 20 B-57s for combat duties in that theatre of operations. These aircraft included 12 'E' versions which had been towing targets. During 1964 and 1965, serious efforts were made to train Vietnamese Air Force crews to operate B-57s, but although some missions were carried out by VNAF crews, and some B-57s

B-57 "G"

appeared in VNAF colours, the experiment was not a success and it was ended in the spring of 1966.

The Vietnam conflict spawned several unconventional versions of the B-57. These included the RB-57E reconnaissance aircraft which, packed with cameras, provided the bombers with the detailed information which they needed of ground concentrations. A total of five of these unarmed aircraft served in the South-East Asia war theatre. They were in fact the longest-operating B-57s there — arriving May 1963 and leaving finally the the middle of 1971.

The B-57G was developed as a night intruder through a conversion of the B-57B. The 'G' was easily identified through a large 'jaw' fitted beneath the nose by the original manufacturer, Martin. This contained a low-light television system and other sensors installed by Westinghouse for the detection of targets at night, and for directing laser-guided bombs. Each aircraft carried four 500lb 'smart' bombs on wing stations for this latter purpose, in addition to other bombs in the bomb bay. The aircraft were equipped with a computer, and bomb drops were automatic after consent from the pilot. Most laser-guided bombs were said to have had an accuracy of 15ft of target. Sixteen B-57s were converted to this configuration at a total cost of $49million. Combat operations with them lasted about two years before the aircraft were withdrawn.

Prior to the Vietnam conflict, four different types of a long-wing 'D' version of the B-57 were developed by Martin for USAF Strategic Air Command as a high-flying reconnaissance machine. Span was 106ft, compared with 64ft of the basic aircraft, and with J57 engines developing 10,000lb thrust in enlarged pods, an operating altitude of over 55,000ft could be achieved, well beyond the range of existing Soviet fighters. The differences in the four types were small and depended on which part of the world they were destined for. B-57s were used for 'spy in the sky' operations in Taiwan, where they appeared in Nationalist Chinese markings,

Left:
B-57G, the ultimate night intruder version with low-light TV and downwards firing Gatling gun.
USAF via R. Mikesh

Below left:
A B-57G model takes off bristling with all-weather weapons system sensors. *USAF via R. Mikesh*

Below:
A Martin RB-57D high altitude reconnaissance variant in 1956. *R. Mikesh*

and in Europe, and were also pressed into service as high-flying targets for USAF fightres, as radiation-samplers in nuclear weapon tests in the Pacific, and for weather reconnaissance.

The long wing produced structural problems and breakages, which resulted in the version being grounded. But Martin strengthened the structure of some, which served with the USAF on test and target missions (coded as EB-57Ds, with modernised electronic countermeasure equipment) until finally scrapped in the middle 1970s.

An even more esoteric version of the longwing B-57, the RB-57F, emerged in the summer of 1963 as the result of a contract placed by the USAF in March 1962 with General Dynamics. Wingspan of the 'F' grew to 122ft with a wing area of 2,000sq ft compared with 960sq ft of the basic version, while the engines were changed to two Pratt and Whitney TF33-P-11A turbofans, each developing 16,000lb thrust, augmented by a pair of P&W J60-P-9 turbojets, one outboard

of the main engines under each wing. These were used to give the 'F' an operational height of well over 60,000ft being air-started following take-off. Thrust was 3,000lb at sea level. The turbojets could be detached for long-range missions. Two B-57Fs were built from scratch under the original contract, and 19 more followed using parts from other B-57s.

'Fs' were used for high-level reconnaissance from Pakistan, the Far East, Europe and many other areas of the world, for weather and nuclear-sampling, and by NASA, equipped with a special pallet in the bomb bay carrying cameras and other equipment, to survey earth resources. In some tasks heights of more than 70,000ft were achieved.

One US version of the Canberra which never got off the ground was what would today be called an executive jet. It was termed a utility courier by Martin who proposed it to the USAF in 1954. There would have been seating for up to 11 passengers, or it could have been used as an ambulance. Tip tanks each holding 600gal would have altered its external shape, and it would have had a redesigned canopy. Martin promoted it as a fast transport for Strategic Air Command bomber crews and went so far as to build a mock-up with four seats and two bunks, but nobody was buying, and the project died.

Below:
A General Dynamics RB-57F in 1964. This variant operated at more than 70,000ft. *NASA via R. Mikesh*

12 Dual control — The T Mk 4

The Canberra T Mk 4 Official Description (Specification T2/49)

Description	Engines
This aircraft is a midwing monoplane and powered by engines mounted in the wings, carrying one instructor, one pupil pilot and one navigator. The fuselage is a stressed skin of semi-monocoque construction, the nose portion being pressurised with hot/cold control. The upper centre fuselage holds fuel tanks 1, 2 and 3, the lower part being the bomb compartment, enclosed by hydraulically retractable doors. The tail portion is of a standard pattern with variable incidence tailplane. Jettisonable tanks are carried on the wing tips, and all tanks are refuelled by ordinary ground methods through large orifices.	*Number:* Two Rolls-Royce jet propelled engines *Type:* Avon Mk 1/RA3 *Dry Weight:* 2,276lb *Engine Rating:* Thrust 6,500lb each engine *Starting:* Rolls-Royce turbostarter by cartridge

Operational Equipment	Dimensions
VHF　　(ARI 5490) Rebecca　　(ARI 5610) Orange Putter　　(ARI 5800) Gee Mk 3　　(ARI 5816) ILS　　(ARI 18011) and Zero Reader IFF Mk 10　　(ARI 5848) Radio Altimeter AYF　　(ARI 5284)	*Span:* 64ft　　*Length:* 65ft 6in *Height:* 15ft 7in *Sweep back $\frac{1}{4}c$:* 13° 33' *Wing thickness chord:* 12% at root 　9% at tip *Track:* 15ft 9in at main wheels *Wheelbase:* (triangular) 14ft fwd of main wheels

Controls	Fuel
Flaps: Split type *Total area:* 73sq ft *Dive Brakes:* Type: finger spoiler, drag channel section. Hydraulically operated *Area:* (inner face of brakes to air stream only) 596.8sq in *Manually operated controls:* Electrically operated for trimming purposes only and electrically operated tailplane Note: Spring tabs are fitted to control surfaces	*Centre fuselage tanks:* No 1 tank　　　　512gal No 2 tank　　　　317gal No 3 tank　　　　545gal Wing tip Jettison tanks 2 tanks, 250gal each　　500gal 　　　　　　Total: 1,874gal *Fuel:* Avtag or Kerosine Engine *oil* capacity — 17pt each engine

With the aerodynamic configuration and main systems of a B2, the T4 was designed to provide a dual control pilot-training role, and for this purpose two pilot stations were designed into the existing nose fuselage with controls and instruments positioned for both pilots to differ as little as possible from the B2 standard.

This resulted in slightly cramped sitting positions for the pupil pilot on the left and the instructor on the right.

Entry into the navigator's station was also complicated by the complex sliding ejector seat of the instructor, and the T4 had, in fact, a congested and complicated crew compartment which was far less convenient than its operational counterparts. However, in flight it performed as well as the operational variants and in some aspects rather better, owing to lower weight.

Although retaining the bomb bay, the trainer was not required for bombing training so that without bomb beams and associated equipment the normal loaded weight was about 7,000lb less than that of the B2 and this resulted in improvements in some aspects of performance.

The prototype T4, WM467, was flown by Beamont from Samlesbury on 12 June 1952, and the livelier performance was put to good use that year at Farnborough in September with WM467 and also at Paris Le Bourget in June 1953 with production T4 WE773; the latter demonstration receiving an especially favourable press.

Prior to introduction of T4s to 231 OCU in 1953 some fatal accidents had begun to appear in the Canberra training system which were not connected to the earlier, and subsequently cured, runaway tailplanes.

In these accidents to B Mk 2s the only common denominator appeared to be that they happened at night or in bad visibility and very soon after take-off or following a go-around, they all involved pilots under conversion training or with low hours on type. Similar accidents and at a higher rate were also occurring in the Meteor training programme.

Below:
Prototype T4 at Warton. *British Aerospace via D. Woods*

Bottom:
The same T4 on test from Warton. *British Aerospace*

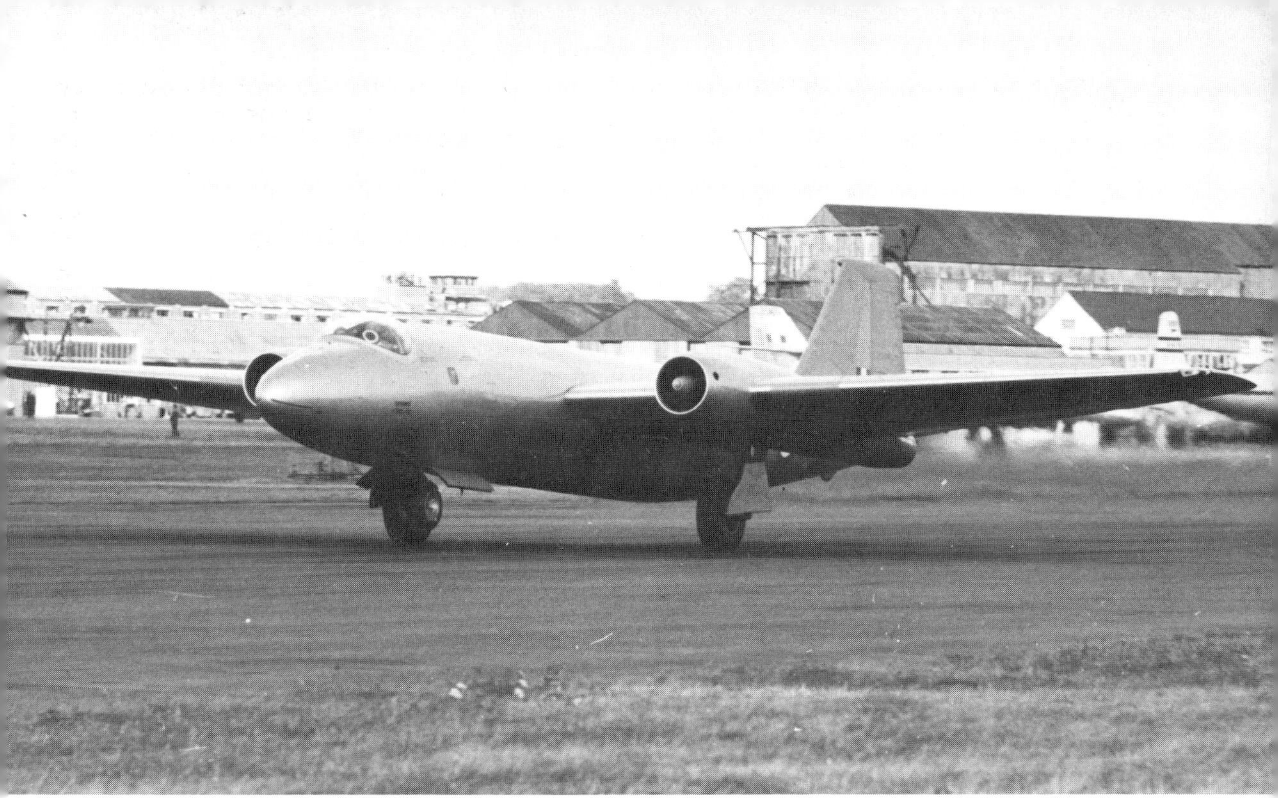

Above:
Prototype T4 at Farnborough display 1953, flown by R. P. Beamont. *D. Woods*

Left:
The navigator's station in a T4 trainer. *British Aerospace*

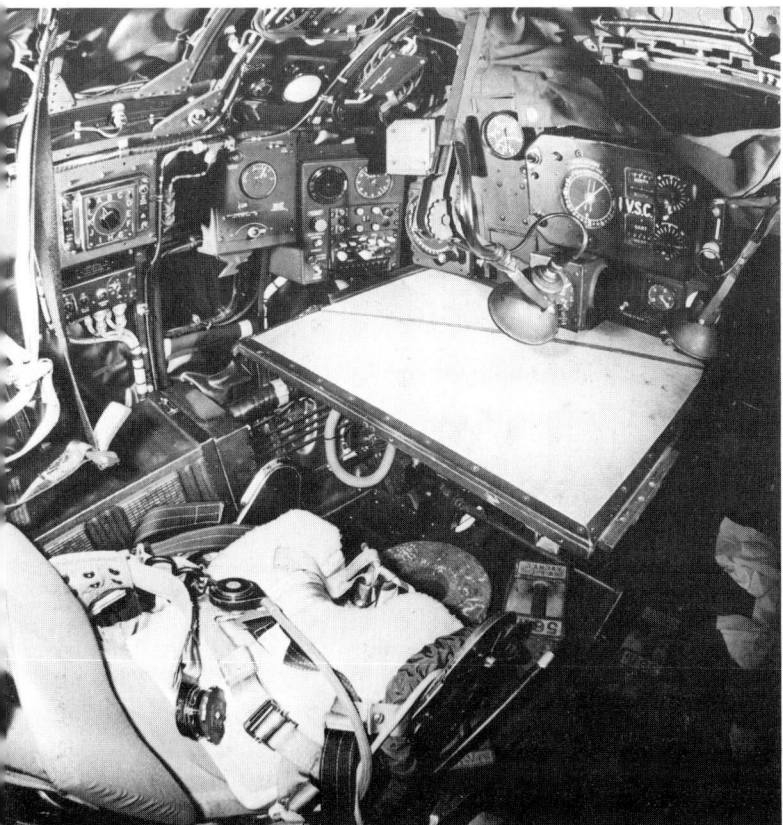

The cause in the case of the Canberras was eventually traced to the much increased rate of horizontal acceleration of these new jets when under maximum power which resulted in the main instrument reference, the artificial horizon, progressively misreading in the nose-up sense. This led inexperienced pilots to believe that they were climbing too steeply after take-off and, correcting nose-down, some flew into the ground within a mile or so of the airfield boundary.

English Electric had identified this danger and warned the Service that this should be carefully considered in training, but such was the general ease of conversion to the Canberra that by 1953 with many hundreds of pilots already passed through Bassingbourn on B2s, a period of over-confidence occurred in which pupils made their first night flights on Canberras with very few prior daytime hours, and sometimes even in poor weather conditions.

The accident rate increased significantly until more stringent procedures were introduced on minimum day hours before nightflying coupled with strict weather requirements for good visibility on the initial night flight.

Subsequent introduction of the trainer at once enabled experienced instructors to monitor these aspects and ensure their pupils' understanding of the critical instrument errors and of the correct remedial procedures, and no further troubles of this nature were experienced after 1954, 231 OCU continuing to operate a uniquely successful training programme, including pilots from many overseas air forces, for the next 25 years.

Below:
More clean aerodynamics — the T4 prototype, with Len Howat and Peter Hillwood.
Photograph by Charles Brown. British Aerospace via D. Woods

13 Photographic Reconnaissance — The PR3

The Canberra PR3 Official Description (Specification PR31/46)

Description

This aircraft is a midwing monoplane, powered by engines mounted in the wings, carrying a crew of 2 who are provided with a means for ejection. The fuselage is a stressed skin of semi-monocoque construction, the nose portion being pressurised with hot/cold control. The upper centre fuselage holds 5 fuel tanks whilst a ventral tank under the first 4 upper tanks occupies the lower front part of the fuselage. The rear lower portion is used for armament. The centre fuselage makes provision for carrying 6 cameras. The rear fuselage follows a standard pattern with electrical variable incidence tailplane, and provision for 1 survey camera and photocells. Refuelling by standard ground methods.

Engines

Number: Two Rolls-Royce jet propelled engines
Type: Avon Mk 1/RA3
Dry Weight: 2,276lb
Engine Rating: Thrust 6,500lb each engine
Starting: Rolls-Royce turbo-starter by cartridge

Operational Equipment

VHF	(ARI 5490)
Rebecca	(AIR 5610)
Gee H	(ARI 5829)
Orange Putter	(ARI 5800)
Green Satin	(ARI 5851)
IFF Mk 10	(ARI 5848)
Radio Compass, Marconi	AD 7092D
Radio Altimeter AYF	(ARI 5284)
Radio Altimeter Mk 6	(ARI 5380)

Dimensions

Span: 64ft   *Length:* 66ft 8in
Height: 15ft 7in
Sweep back to $\frac{1}{4}c$: 13° 33'
Wing thickness chord:
12% at root
 9% at tip
Track: 15ft 9in at main wheels
Wheelbase: (triangular) 15ft 3in fwd of main wheels

Armament

Cameras: Day Role: 6×F52 and 1×F49
  Alternative Role: 4×F52 and 1×F49
  Survey Day Role: 1×F49
  Night Role: 2×F89, Photocells and 1.75 photoflash crate
Total fuselage fuel weight=15,336lb
Maximum armament load=3,000lb+cameras

Fuels

Centre Fuselage Tanks	Gal
Nos 1 and 2 tanks, 260 ea	520
Nos 3 and 4 tanks, 220 ea	440
No 5 tank	540
Ventral tank (No 6)	417
Wing tip Jettison tanks 2 tanks, 250gal ea	500
	Total: 2,417

Fuel: Avtag or Kerosine
Engine *oil* capacity: 17pt ea

Controls

Flaps: Split type   *Total area:* 73sq ft
Dive Brakes: Type: finger spoiler, drag channel section. Hydraulically operated
Area: (inner face of brakes to air steam only) 596.8sq in
Manually operated controls: Electrically operated for trimming purposes only and electrically operated tailplane
Note: Spring tabs are fitted to control surfaces
Autopilot: Smiths Mk 9

Basically a B5/47 (B2) the PR3 incorporated a 14in extension to the front fuselage to accommodate an additional fuel tank, a camera bay, and a flare bay.

The latter contained seven day/night cameras and a 3,000lb maximum load of flares.

With a crew of two it was intended that the PR version would have speed and altitude capability similar to the B2 bomber version, but with range much increased by the addition of 543gal of internal fuel; but some problems were encountered resulting in delayed CA Release which was finally achieved in early 1953.

PR3 prototype VX181 was flown from Samlesbury by Peter Hillwood on 19 March 1950, and very soon comparative handling trials at Warton revealed a serious increase in vibration levels such that Beamont reported that this configuration could not be cleared to the CA Release limits of the B2.

Problems of this nature had been anticipated since the '8-cycle' incipient flutter of the first prototype VN799 had not been fully cured but only delayed to an acceptable speed range by the various modifications to the elevator circuit, and the 14in extension to the fuselage of the PR3 coupled with redistributed mass had been expected to result at least in increased airframe roughness.

This was now happening and despite recommendations from Warton Flight Operations that a Mach number limit of 0.75 should be set for further flying without modification (compared with 0.84 for the B2), a management decision was taken to send VX181 to Boscombe Down for its first preview in that state in an attempt to keep to programme dates.

Above:
PR3 prototype VX181 at Warton before delivery for Boscombe trials. *British Aerospace*

Above right:
VX181 flying over the Isle of Wight on test from Boscombe Down. *British Aerospace*

Right:
VX181 on trials from Boscombe Down, over the Needles. *British Aerospace*

In very short order Boscombe rejected the PR and returned it to Warton saying that the vibration levels were unacceptable, and this was followed by an extensive investigation of the aerodynamic and mass balance parameters of the elevators in relation to the natural frequency characteristics of the longer PR fuselage.

B. O. (Ollie) Heath, director of advanced engineering at Warton in 1982 and senior stressman in the 1945-55 period recalled that this rejection by Boscombe resulted in a concentrated campaign on all the outstanding vibration areas, Ray Creasey and Ron Dickson both being diverted to it for a time from their specialist swept-wing development work for the future P1 and Lightning.

All five flying prototypes were resonance-tested in the 25 Hangar 'mechanical test' section at Warton, and these tests established the nature of the roughness which led to the waveform vibrations felt at the cockpit as '8-cycle'.

The mechanism was that the fuselage was stiff but the tail unit moved considerably under the excitation provided by turbulence and aerodynamic buffet; and that this when coupled with incipient flutter from marginally balanced elevators and tabs all added up to an unsatisfactorily 'loose' tail-end.

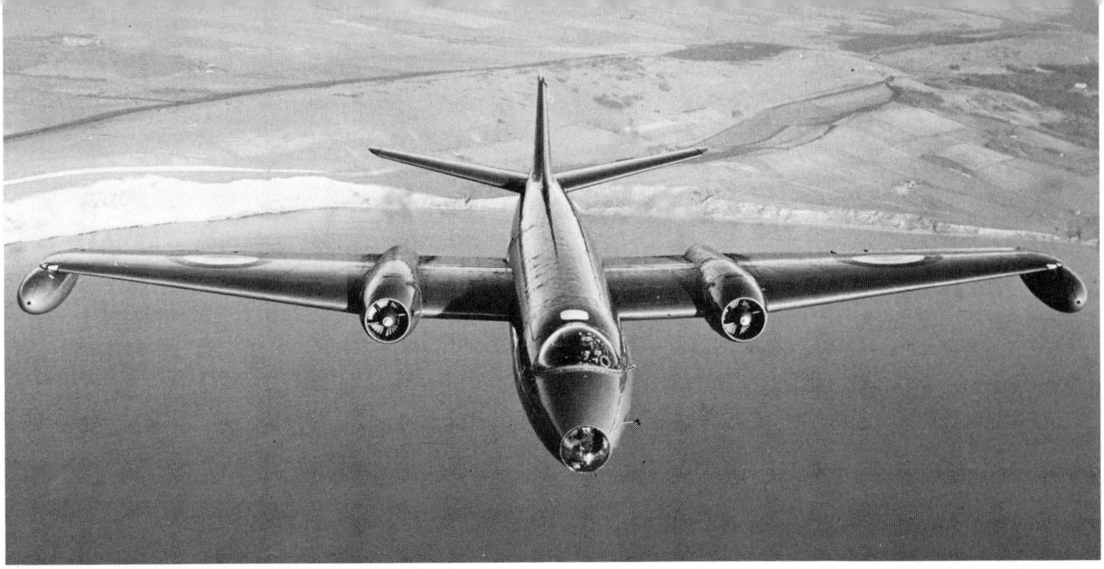

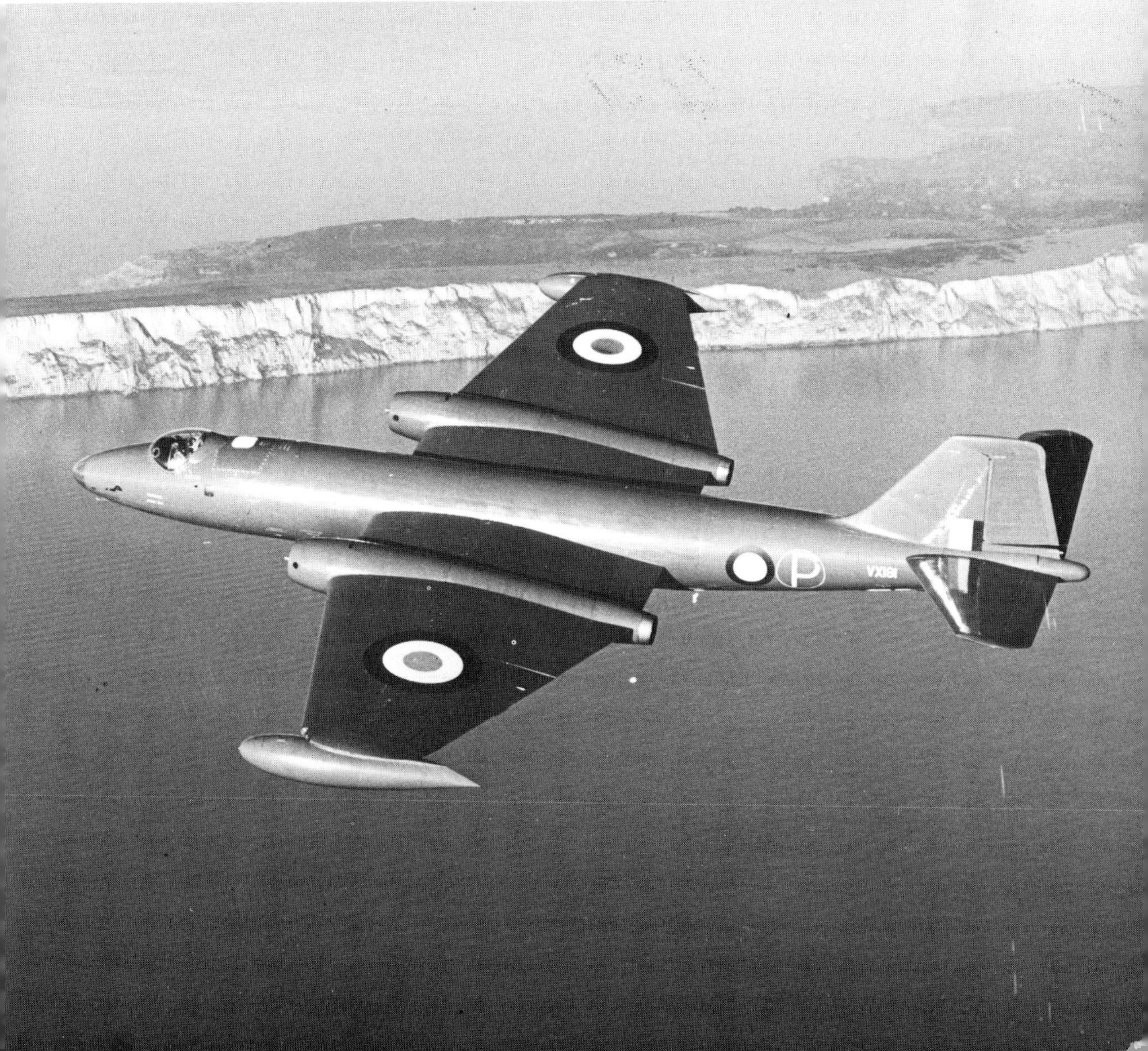
P
VX181

The initial improvements to aerodynamic and mass balancing for the first prototype had provided safe clearance to 500kts IAS and to M0.84 for the B2; but the longer fuselage of the PR3 and its new split elevator system introduced an additional harshness measured at 24cps, and it was while these investigations were still in progress that the chief production test pilot Johnny Squier encountered the first major flight incident when testing production PR3 WE138 at 480kts IAS at 2,000ft.

A sudden onset of 24cps vibration became divergent and violent until, with a bang, something broke and the aircraft pitched up.

Squier slowed down in a climb to 10,000ft and finding the aircraft controllable returned to Samlesbury where, when slowing down on the approach to land, he found sluggish response to elevator and eventually landed rather heavily.

On coming to a standstill the yoke then went right forward instead of aft as it should have under the effect of the elevator mass balance, and it was found that the divergent 24cps flutter had broken off one of the elevator mass balance weights and damaged the elevator cross-shaft assembly, leaving only one side of the elevator properly connected to the pilot!

Further cleaning up of shroud gaps and increases in elevator and tab mass balances to the practical limits did not completely cure the problem which was never fully eliminated, but sufficient improvement to achieve CA Release was eventually obtained by the unpopular and untidy additional method of stiffening the rear fuselage by 'overslabbing' plates on the sides.

This modification standard was introduced to the first production aircraft WE135 before delivery to No 541 Squadron at Benson, and this signalled the beginning of another extraordinary successful chapter of Canberra operations, this time in the PR role, for the RAF from 1953 until disbandment of the last squadron of operational Canberras on 29 May 1982, No 39 Squadron (PR9s) at Wyton.

Top:
First production PR3, WE135, at Warton.
British Aerospace

Above:
PR3 VX181 takes off at Farnborough in 1952; pilot R. P. Beamont. *D. Woods*

14 Specification B22/48 Canberra B Mk 5 and B Mk 6

The second prototype PR3 was converted to this specification into a prototype B5, and this aircraft (VX185) was flown in its new form for the first time on 6 July 1951 by Johnny Squier from Samlesbury.

Originally intended as a target-marker with improved radar and clearance for increased low-level performance, the Mk 5 was actually built for visual bomb/flare aiming with a crew of three and the standard bomb-sight station in the nose as, once again, the radar system development had fallen behind schedule.

Significant changes however were integral leading edge fuel tanks providing 900gal additional fuel, and later with first flight on 15 July 1952, Avon Mk 109 (RA7) engines giving 7,500lb st (1,000lb more than the RA3), and Dunlop's 'Maxaret' anti-skid wheel braking system.

This configuration was put into an intensive test programme with special emphasis on the revised fuel system which was expected to, and did, produce problems associated with spreading fuel out along the wing leading edges which became very cold in prolonged high altitude flight.

By early August 1952, tests had established the conditions under which fuel 'waxing' occurred, and while a cure was sought the flying programme was continued safely on the measurement of performance with the new-standard engines by using a fuel drill involving consumption of the leading-edge fuel first before it had time to cool too far.

The RA7 engines had achieved full handling clearance within four weeks and it was in this phase that long-range proving flights began.

These involved progressively longer sorties to establish range capability, systems reliability and oil and oxygen consumption rates over four to five hours at 40,000 to 50,000ft.

After a while flying round and round the British Isles began to seem rather repetitive to the Warton team, and a suggestion was put forward that some more realistic experience could be gained by doing some of the range flying in a more or less straight line. Gibraltar might be one practical possibility, or alternatively Gander in Newfoundland or Goose Bay in Labrador.

Below:
The first and only B Mk 5. This aircraft was used for the first double Atlantic flight in one day. *British Aerospace*

Sir George Nelson wishes R. P. Beamont well in front of VX185 before the double-Atlantic flight.
British Aerospace

Of these the 1,800nm to Gander was a suitable sector distance for the tests with adequate reserves for diversion, and this became the focus for planning.

At this point, since with average westerly headwinds the outbound sector was going to take about 4hr 30min and the return sector up to one hour less, it was suggested that it would be quite practical to make the return flight the same day; and this was where the news media became interested!

The Royal Aero Club was anxious to observe the flight for record purposes, but said that as it had to be between capital cities according to their rules, the route would have to be Belfast to St John's, Newfoundland. So, as they would not accept the EEC's counter-proposition that Preston was the capital of the North-west, and because the St John's runway was too short in any case, a compromise was arrived at that the flight would take off from Aldergrove and overfly Gander to Gander Lake which was considered by the RAeC to be the equivalent distance to St John's.

Now the battle was on because although Warton thought that it was merely carrying out the next interesting stage in the test programme, everyone else seemed to think of it as the magical 'double Atlantic flight'.

Of course this had never been done before, but to many thousands of ferry pilots in the war and airline pilots since the Atlantic crossing was scarcely magical in their 10-12hr one-way stints. So Warton attempted to keep things in perspective.

The working-up trials proceeded well in typical Canberra fashion and on 21 August VX185 made a final triangular proving flight from Warton to the East Atlantic weather ship, to Manston, to the Orkneys and back to Warton; a distance of approximately 1,200nm in 3.05hr.

During this flight which proved mechanically uneventful most of the first hour and a half to the westerly turning point and back up-Channel over Cornwall was flown in sight of a massive electrical storm build-up, with a giant 'anvil' head which was well above the Canberra's cruising height of 44,000ft as it

penetrated the turbulent top layer over Devon. This evil-looking black and yellow cloud mass below was constantly illuminated by flashing lighting and was one of the most violent storm scenes in Beamont's experience. On landing back at Warton the first news was coming in of the Lynmouth disaster in which the town was being partly washed away with much loss of life as the Canberra flew overhead at 44,000ft.

But the tests on VX185 were complete and go-ahead was given for the Atlantic sortie.

With Peter Hillwood as second pilot who would fly the return leg, and Dennis Watson the Company Chief Navigator, VX185 was

Crew aboard — dawn on 26 August 1952.
British Aerospace

74

positioned at Aldergrove on the evening of 25 August. The forecast for the following day indicated reasonable landing weather at each end and an average headwind westbound of 40kts or so which was acceptable.

Beamont briefed the Press who were now present in large numbers, and arranged for a 6.30am take-off the following morning.

At 4am the weather briefing had almost inevitably changed and while Gander weather was likely to stay open, frontal activity was now expected to affect Aldergrove later in the day. Of more significance however the Atlantic system now showed promise of 60-70kts headwinds at a high tropopause level of 40-41,000ft over much of the route.

Any height gain above the tropopause could be expected to reduce the effective headwind by 5kts/1,000ft, and so knowing the altitude capabilities of the aircraft Beamont decided to go, especially as the forecaster could only suggest worsening conditions over the next few days.

Watson had insufficient time to revise the navigation plan before going out on schedule to crew the aircraft, and he completed it after take-off.

In the cold, misty dawn on the aerodrome visibility was adequate though poor, and immediately on this high-humidity morning the canopy steamed over completely. This caused some problems after start-up when taxying before the demisting hot air system, which was never a strong point in Canberras, began to take effect.

Final systems checks on the runway were all satisfactory and at 6.34am Beamont began the take-off roll at an aircraft weight of 47,355lb of which 23,672lb was fuel.

After a quick turn round the airfield at full power, course was set at 6.35 at 400kts over the RAeC timing point on the runway and the Canberra pulled up to climb at full power

Above:
Cleaning dew off the canopy.
British Aerospace

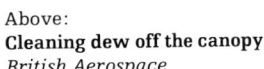

Left:
VX185 takes off for Gander and return, August 1952.
British Aerospace

Below left:
185 taxies in at Gander.
British Aerospace

entering the overcast at 800ft and breaking clear eventually at 34,000ft.

The technique used was a 400kts climb to M0.76, continuing at full power to the M0.76/weight ceiling, and then stabilising a cruise-climb at max continuous power at M0.76.

This was commenced after a shallow descent from the full-power ceiling, and levelled initially at 42,700ft/M076/212kts/IAS. ·

Maintaining M0.76 VX185 was kept at the absolute weight-ceiling for this condition, using max continuous power for each hour and then full power for the permissible period before returning to max continuous.

By 7.46hr the cruise had reached 45,000ft and in anticipation of benefiting from the falling wind gradient (but having no means of positively establishing this!) speed was increased to M0.775.

Wing leading-edge fuel was consumed first to 100/100gal to eliminate risk of usable fuel loss by 'waxing', and the established fuel drills were operated satisfactorily throughout the flight.

At an early stage navigation facilities began to become meagre with the failure of Loran APN9, API Mk II and AMLI Mk IV. This left the compass, VHF, a trial-installation radio compass and the navigator's pencil, and with only sporadic radio compass bearings and in the event no help in VHF from the two Atlantic weather ships, Watson was quite fully occupied for the first 1,500 miles!

The autopilot had also become unserviceable so the whole operation was hand-flown, but the fine handling qualities of the Canberra enabled this quite precise cruise-climb to be flown with accuracy and courses to be steered to an average which caused unusually complimentary remarks from the navigator to the effect that, 'It's nice to see the course held to $\pm\frac{1}{2}°$!'

A height of 46,000ft was reached at 8.33hr, and the Canberra was still flying in the grey dawn light with an unbroken cloud layer below at about 40,000ft, and it was cold in the cabin. There was no turbulence, the cloud horizon ahead was sharp-edged against limitless visibility and the Canberra with engines quietly humming at max continuous power was precisely balanced in trim and needed no more than finger tips on the wheel to keep in steady on climb-speed and course.

There had been no VHF contact with the first weather ship and only fleeting radio compass bearings, insufficient for a reliable running fix, so that good contact with the second ship, 'Ocean Station Coca' about 600nm east of Newfoundland, was becoming important.

Watson raised radio compass contact at about 150nm but it was again intermittent and insufficient for a reliable fix. Estimating passing within 90nm to the North it was intended to obtain VHF contact and a radar fix, but again without success.

Beamont continued to call on VHF without effect until a voice suddenly replied saying he was Air Canada Argonaut 531 and that he could not raise 'Coca' either, but could he help. Beamont replied saying no thanks but it was nice to talk to somebody. Then the Argonaut pilot said 'Canberra, is that right that you are turning right round at Gander and going back to UK?'

The Canberra crew thought, 'fame at last — he's been reading the papers', and confirmed it. There was a pause and then the Canadian mid-Atlantic voice said, 'Gee — what a helluva way to spend a day!' as he ploughed on eastwards somewhere down below in all the weather.

So VX185 continued on its way, now holding level at 47,000ft and allowing Mach number to build up to 0.8 as the fuel weight continued to reduce.

Then at 9.55hr Watson raised St John's beacon 20° on the port beam for long enough to establish a running fix which put the Canberra only slightly north of planned track. However, assuming that with the known weather system the wind would tend to back and give any cross-track error to starboard, a 5° course alteration to port was made at an estimated 300 miles out from Fogo Island.

On reaching the planned let-down point at 200nm estimated from Gander breaks began to appear in the cloud cover ahead with golden dawn sunlight now on it, and as the Canberra nosed down through the cirrus at 38,000ft and M0.81, land could just be seen on the horizon ahead.

With a further port course correction landfall was reached and identified approximately 16nm north of track, and so on over the rock and conifer landscape of Newfoundland in gin-clear visibility with the early morning sun throwing contrasting shadows through the broken cumulus below to the wide expanse of the ex-military airfield of Gander.

Limiting Mach number was converted to the IAS test limit of 500kts over the last few miles down to 500ft over the Gander Lake where the Royal Aero Club official observer was waiting patiently in a small motor boat.

Peter Hillwood had come forward from his ejection seat in the navigator's compartment and, standing by Beamont's right shoulder to see the arrival, had an interesting experience of the airframe buffet at limiting Mach when not strapped in or supported in any way — a procedure which would be somewhat frowned upon today!

Throttled back over the deep blue lake VX185 curved back into the airport circuit with the crew enjoying the limitless visibility of this morning-sun-lit Newfoundland scene, and touched down at 11.12hr BST for a recorded point-to-point time of 4.34hr.

The ever-enthusiastic and efficient English Electric support party took over the aircraft, and the hospitable airport officials insisted on taking the crew some miles off the base for a 'relaxed meal'. This was enjoyed by Hillwood and Watson while Beamont stayed at the terminal briefing office to study the forecast and clear the return flight plan.

Eventually catching up with the lunch party (breakfast time for the Gander people), Beamont had just started on a massive steak when the telephone reported, 'VX185 ready for flight'.

Another perilous dash down dirt roads through the towering fir forest, and the crew were soon shutting the Canberra's cockpit hatch, the inside by now heated to oven level by the clear August sun. Just at this point a car drew up with a squeal of tyres and with much gesticulation indicated that the hatch be opened again. When this was done a face

said, 'You can't go away without a present from Canada', and in came three large packages each containing a whole smoked salmon. Then with these highly-aromatic items stowed on the floor, as there was nowhere else for them, engines were started, this time with Hillwood at the wheel.

The Met briefing coupled with the outbound experience had confirmed the tropopause height and jetstream, and so for this sector it was decided to fly a similar great circle plan but this time levelling at 41,000ft and cruising with benefit of a high average tailwind at M0.8 initially and increasing as the fuel weight reduced.

Taking off at 13.10hr BST after this longer-than-intended turnround and setting initial course for Gander Lake to overfly the still patient RAeC observer at 500kts, VX185 was turned straight into a max power climb on the first heading on course for UK.

The weather was sparkling clear, giving a magnificent view of the lakes and coastline in the morning sun as the Canberra climbed fast towards the line of cloud still on the eastern horizon where it had been in the morning.

Estimated time for this sector announced by Watson as he finished his calculations soon after take-off was 3.30hr, and this time there was to be benefit from positive navigational checks. Running ADF fixes were obtained on St John's, on both weather ships and on Bush Mills in Ireland so that it was possible to fly an accurate track and also to confirm that the jetstream was helping to as much as 130mph part of the time. Watson began to predict a fast time and once again the Canberra was performing perfectly.

At the end of the second hour M0.805 was being maintained level at 7,000rpm and

Below:
Landing back at Aldergrove after 10hr 3min.
British Aerospace

42,000ft, and during the third hour speed was increased to M0.81 at 40,000ft using 7,300rpm. Without the need to cruise-climb at the weight ceiling there was also no need to use max continuous power after the first hour, or combat power at all, to maintain this high cruising speed.

A significant change in this sector was the sun relationship. On the flight out the sunrise had not caught up sufficiently to warm the cockpit by solar radiation, and all the crew had become uncomfortably cold. But on this return leg which started with a hot cockpit and the sun high on the starboard beam, the first hour was comfortably warm.

However on an easterly heading at a groundspeed reaching at times over 600mph the sun disappeared rapidly behind the starboard wing and after two hours was providing very little warmth for the crew. This was an early experience of sustained jet speeds 'away' from the sun and of the very short eastbound day soon to become normal experience to jet airline travellers, and it was strange to have left the early-morning sun at Gander and to be descending towards UK with a late-afternoon sun low on the horizon behind only 3hr later.

The last hour had been through the turbulent tops of high cloud, and at 150nm from the Irish coast good VHF bearings were obtained from Aldergrove which enabled Watson to monitor Nutts Corner beacon signals and plan a fast letdown through reported unfavourable weather to a safe cloud-break over Lough Neagh, in order to avoid a slow procedure descent and GCA (ground-controlled approach)

This worked out well and Hillwood broke cloud in rain and low visibility with five miles to go to Aldergrove, with radio clearance to

Right:
185 back home at Warton on 26 August 1952 with, left to right: Atkinson, Page, Eaves, Pickthall, Watson, Shorrock, Hollock, RPB, Hothersal, Hillwood.
British Aerospace

cross immediately at low level for RAeC timing.

Landing in a downpour of rain at 16.39 BST the flight from Gander had taken 3.26hr point-to-point for 1,818nm and had consumed 1,747gal fuel.

The round journey had taken 10hr 3min and VX185 was in fully serviceable condition except for the failed navigation equipments, and it did not need refuelling for the short flight home through the rain over the Irish Sea which was made as soon as the crew could decently disengage from the throng of Press and well-wishers at Aldergrove.

On landing back at Warton at about 18.30 BST after what had been quite a busy day there was a small but enthusiastic group on the tarmac including the wives of the crew — small because it was after normal working hours and in the North-west things are kept in perspective, and enthusiastic because the media had apparently been active all day and even the BBC and broken into programmes with bulletins on, 'where the Atlantic fliers were'.

After brief formalities a discussion began over the technicalities of what had been a significant technical achievement by any standards, and the main points were summarised later in the report on the flight.

'Canberra B Mk 5, No VX185, was flown from Aldergrove Northern Ireland, to Gander

Above:
Nose detail of the Mk 5 showing the revised optically flat bombaimer's window.
British Aerospace

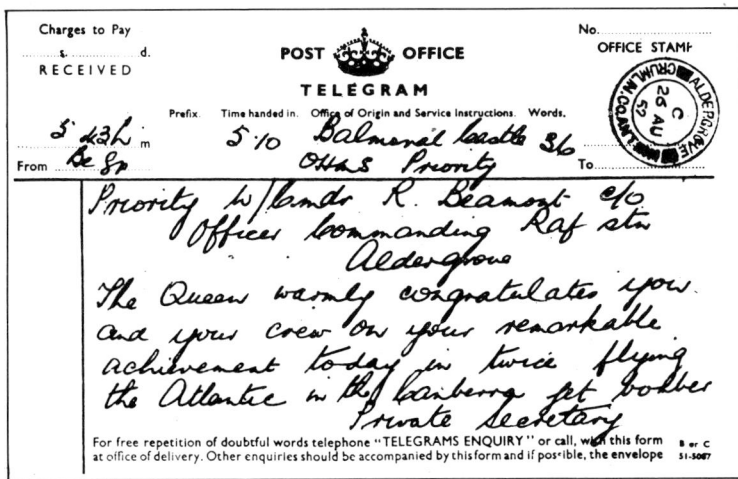

Left:
Telegram from HM The Queen, 26 August 1952.

Newfoundland and return to Aldergrove on 26 August in 10hr 3min elapsed time.

'Operating conditions were satisfactory throughout in respect of controllability, aircraft and engine serviceability and seat comfort.

'Cockpit heating was found to be inadequate in these conditions and would clearly be inadequate for night operation.

'The scale of navigational equipment carried would have been adequate if it had all remained serviceable.

'In this aircraft hand-flying over long distances is a pleasant and relaxed activity . . .'

During the discussion with Managing Director Freddy Page and Chief Engineer Don Crowe and others, someone came in with a buff envelope and said, 'It's for Mr Beamont'. Later as the meeting broke up Beamont remembered the envelope and opened it — it was a telegram from the Queen.

In its trials the Mk 5 was completely successful but although the target-marker role was dropped and this mark was not ordered for production, advantage was taken of the improvements for a production series of Mk 2s converted to leading-edge fuel, Avon RA7 engines and Maxaret brakes known as the B Mk 6; and also for one squadron of these aircraft fitted additionally with a ventral 4×20mm gunpack and underwing pylons for bombs or Matra rocket launchers, known as the B(I)6.

This series introduced the low-level 'interdictor' role to RAF Germany and paved the way for the B(I)8 to follow.

Top right:
First production B Mk 6 at Warton. *British Aerospace*

Centre right:
A B Mk 6 on test from Samlesbury.

Bottom right:
A B(I) Mk 6 over the Pennines showing the ventral gun pack and a 1,000lb bomb on the wing pylon. *British Aerospace*

Canberra B Mk 6 Official Description

Description	Engines
This aircraft is a midwing monoplane and powered by engines mounted in the wings, carrying a crew of 3 who are provided with a means for ejection. The fuselage is a stressed skin of semi-monocoque construction, the nose portion being pressurised with hot/cold control. The upper centre fuselage holds fuel tanks 1, 2 and 3 the lower part being the bomb compartment, enclosed by hydraulically retractable doors. The tail portion is of a standard pattern with variable incidence tailplane. Provision is made for a 300gal LR tank in the bomb bay and jettisonable tanks are carried on the wing tips. Refuelling of all tanks is by ordinary ground methods, through large orifices.	*Number:* Two Rolls-Royce jet propelled engines *Type:* Avon Mk 109/RA7 *Dry Weight:* 2,460lb *Rating:* Thrust 7,500lb each engine *Starting:* Rolls-Royce turbostarter by cartridge

Operational Equipment	Dimensions
VHF (ARI 5490) Rebecca (ARI 5610) Gee H (ARI 5829) IFF Mk 10 (ARI 5848) Orange Putter (ARI 5800) Radio Altimeter AYF (ARI 5284) ILS (ARI 18011) and Zero Reader Radio Compass, Marconi AD7092D Blue Shadow (ARI 5856) can be fitted to S00	*Span:* 64ft *Length:* 65ft 6in *Height:* 15ft 7in *Sweep back at $\frac{1}{4}c$:* 13° 33' *Wing thickness chord:* 12% at root 9% at tip *Track:* 15ft 9in at main wheels *Wheelbase:* (triangular) 14' fwd of main wheels

Armament	Fuel
1×5,000lb HC or 2×4,000lb HC or 6×1,000lb bombs With roles for the above 1×F24 camera or Low-level Night Photographic role, 2×F97 Mk 2 cameras and photoflashes, or Target role, 300gal bomb bay tank with 3×1,000lb target bombs or Window launcher Total fuselage fuel weight=11,280lb Maximum bomb load=10,000lb. With this load acceleration is slightly reduced	*Centre fuselage tanks:* No 1 tank 535gal No 2 tank 325gal No 3 tank 540gal *Wing* Integral tanks Port/Stbd, 450gal each 900gal *Wing* tip jettison tanks, 244gal each 488gal Total 2,788gal

Controls	
Flaps: Split type *Total area:* 73sq ft *Dive brakes:* Type: finger spoiler, drag channel section. Hydraulically operated *Area:* (inner face of brakes to air stream only) 596.8sq in *Manually operated controls:* Electrically operated for trimming purposes only and electrically operated tailplane Note: Spring tabs are fitted to control surfaces	*Fuel* — Avtag or Kerosine Engine *oil* capacity — 13.6pt each 300gal fuel tank can be fitted in bomb bay if required

15 Reconnaissance Development — The PR7

Canberra PR7 Official Description

Description	Engines
This aircraft is a midwing monoplane powered by engines mounted in the wings, carrying a crew of 2 who are provided with a means for ejection. The fuselage is a stressed skin of semi-monocoque construction, the nose portion being pressurised with hot/cold control. The upper centre fuselage holds 5 fuel tanks, whilst a ventral tank under the first 4 upper tanks occupies the lower front part of the fuselage. The rear lower portion is used for armament. The centre fuselage makes provision for carrying 6 cameras. The rear fuselage follows a standard pattern with electrical variable incidence tailplane, and provision for 1 survey camera and photocells. Refuelling by standard ground methods.	*Number:* Two Rolls-Royce jet propelled engines *Type:* Avon Mk 109/RA7 *Dry weight:* 2,460lb *Ratin:* Thrust 7,500lb each engine *Starting:* Rolls-Royce turbostarter by cartridge

Operational Equipment

VHF (ARI 5490)	ILS (ARI 18011) and Zero Reader	
Rebecca (ARI 5610)		
Gee H (ARI 5829)	IFF Mk 10 (ARI 5848)	
Orange Putter (ARI 5800)	Radio Compass, Marconi AD 7092D	
Radio Altimeter AYF (ARI 5284)	High level radio altimeter	
Green Satin (ARI 5851)	Mk 6 (ARI 5380)	

Dimensions

Span: 64ft   *Length:* 66ft 8in
Height: 15ft 7in
Sweep back at $\frac{1}{4}c$: 13° 33'
Wing thickness chord:
12% at root
9% at tip
Track: 15ft 9in at main wheels
Wheelbase: (triangular) 15ft 3in fwd of main wheels

Armament

Cameras:
Day role: 6×F52 and 1×F49
Alternative role: 4×F52 and 1×F49
Survey Day role: 1×F49
Night role: 2×F89, photocells and 3×16½″ flashes
Low-level Night role: 2×F97, photocells and 1.75 photoflash crate
Total fuselage fuel weight=15,336lb
Maximum armament load=3,000lb+cameras

Controls

Flaps: Split type
Total area: 73sq ft
Dive Brakes: Type: finger spoiler, drag channel section. Hydraulically operated
Area: (inner face of brakes to air stream only) 596.8sq in
Autopilot: Smiths Mk 9
Manually operated controls: Electrically operated for trimming purposes only and electrically operated tailplane
Note: Spring tabs are fitted to control surfaces

Fuel

	Gal
Centre fuselage tanks	
Nos 1 and 2 tanks, 260 ea	520
Nos 3 and 4 tanks, 220 ea	440
No 5 tank	540
Ventral tank (No 6)	417
Wing integral (Port and Stbd, 450gal each)	900
Wing tip jettison tanks 2 tanks, 244gal each	488
Total:	3,305

Fuel: Avtag or Kerosine
Engine *oil* capacity — 13.6pt each

The successful introduction of the PR3 was soon followed by development of the PR7 with Avon RA7 engines, wing leading edge fuel tanks and Maxaret anti-skid brakes.

There was no prototype as most of the changes had already been cleared on VX185, the Mk 5 prototype, and the first production aircraft — WH773 — was flown at Samlesbury on 28 October 1953. This mark was to remain the backbone of RAF photo-reconnaissance for more than 20 years, but during the early 1950s the high-altitude potential of the Canberra was seen to be ripe for further exploitation.

This was a period in which extreme altitude was seen to be an assurance against interception from any source, and in the USA Lockheed were evolving the U-2 series while Martin and General Dynamics worked on developments of the Martin-built Canberra for this role.

Accordingly English Electric received a contract in 1953 for a development of the PR7 with Avon 206 (RA24) engines of 11,250lb st to reach an 'operational height' exceeding 60,000ft and to be called the High Altitude PR9.

Since standard B2s, PR3s and 7s could readily exceed 50,000ft (one on test having exceeded 54,000ft) this did not seem too difficult, although it was felt that some increase in wing area would be needed to reduce the wing loading significantly. Here design thinking became concerned that a simple extension of wing span could be

Below:
A PR7 on test showing the nose-fuselage camera bays.
British Aerospace

Bottom:
The PR7. *British Aerospace*

counter-productive by reducing the already restrictive Mach trim and buffet limits of about M0.84. So the favoured solution was to increase the wing area by a small increase in span and an substantial increase in chord at the centre section between the engine nacelle and fuselage and thus so it was hoped, improving the compressibility boundary by effectively reducing the thickness/chord ratio. But unfortunately it did not turn out this way.

After initial design work at Warton, Napier's at Luton were subcontracted to modify PR7 WH793 as a prototype for the engine and wing changes, and this configuration was flown on 8 July 1955 at Cranfield by Napier's chief test pilot Mike Randrup with flight engineer Walter Shirley as test observer.

After an initial assessment by Beamont at Cranfield the aircraft was brought to Warton for its test programme and it was soon found that although the great increase in power provided by the RA24s gave remarkable climb performance up to 50,000ft, the rate of climb dropped off rapidly above that and it was apparent that either engine thrust was lower than specification at altitude or else airframe drag was up.

Intensive testing over the rest of the year gradually brought the conclusion that the

Right:
HA PR9 prototype with large RA24 engine nacelles, on an early assessment flight from Warton, 19 September 1956.
British Aerospace

Below:
RPB poses the new planform for the photographic Meteor.
British Aerospace

Below right:
The new wing shape seen from above on the old (PR7) fuselage.
British Aerospace

induced drag from the new centre section at the high incidence of high altitude flight was nearly absorbing the increased thrust margin; and although 55,000ft could be reached with a reasonable operational load, the highest point achieved was 59,800ft on 18 September 1956 by Beamont who said that it was barely climbing there and with only just enough fuel left to get home!

This was a disappointment, particularly as it was known that developments of the Martin Canberra B-57 in two stages of increase in wing span and engine power were achieving operating heights approaching 70,000ft.

Nevertheless the rugged general potential of this powerful PR aircraft was still considered valuable, and procurement was continued of the production version.

This had a redesigned nose similar in layout to the B(I)8 but with an opening pilot's canopy (the only British variant with this which was a major improvement for operation in hot climates).

Access to the navigator's forward station was also improved by entry through a sideways-opening nose section, and the navigator was subsequently provided with an ejector seat from the 2nd production aircraft onwards.

It was in tests of the first aircraft of this series, XH129 which had been built by Short Bros and made its first flight on 27 July 1958, that trouble occurred.

Above:
Pressure breathing helmet and partial pressure jerkin for the trials on WH793 which reached approx 60,000ft on 23 November 1956. *British Aerospace*

Right:
The pressure helmet is a tight fit in the cockpit. *British Aerospace*

Canberra HA PR9 Official Description

Description	Engines
This aircraft is a midwing monoplane with engines mounted in the wings, and carries a crew of 2. The fuselage is a stressed skin of semi-monocoque construction, the nose portion being pressurised with hot/cold control. The upper centre fuselage holds 5 fuel tanks whilst a ventral tank under the first 4 upper tanks occupies the lower front part of the fuselage. The rear lower portion is used for armament. The centre fuselage makes provision for carrying 6 cameras. The rear fuselage follows a standard pattern with electrical variable incidence tailplane and provision for 1 survey camera and photocells. Refuelling is by standard ground methods.	*Number:* Two Rolls-Royce jet propelled engines *Type:* Avon RA24 *Dry Weight:* 3,045lb *Rating:* Thrust 11,250lb each engine *Starting:* Propyl Nitrate

Operational Equipment

VHF   (ARI 5490)
Gee H   (ARI 5829) or Blue Study + Gee Mk 3
Orange Putter   (ARI 5800)
Green Satin   (ARI 5851)
Radio Altimeter Mk 5   (ARI 5378)
Radio Altimeter Mk 6   (ARI 5380)
ILS   (ARI 18011)

Armament

High and Medium Altitude PR Role
4×F96 cameras and 1×F49   or
4×F52 cameras and 1×F49
High Altitude Night Role
3×F89 Mk 3 cameras and 2 PECs operated by 5×8in or 3×16½in photo flashes
Low Altitude Night Role
2×F97 cameras
Total fuselage fuel weight=15,336lb
Maximum armament load=3,000lb+cameras

Controls

Flaps: Split type   *Total area:* 73sq ft
Dive Brakes: Type: finger spoilter, drag channel section. Hydraulically operated
Area: (inner face of brakes to air stream only) 596.8sq in
Autopilot: Smiths Mk 10
Rudder: Hydraulically operated with electrical autostabiliser
Manually operated controls: Electrically operated for trimming purposes only and electrically operated tailplane
Note: Spring tabs are fitted to control surfaces

Dimensions

Span: 68ft   *Length:* 66ft 8in
Height: 15ft 7in
Sweep back at $\frac{1}{4}$*c:* 13° 33'
Wing thickness chord:
10.3% at root
8% at tip
Track: 15' 9" at main wheels
Wheelbase: (triangular) 15ft 3in fwd of main wheels

Fuel

Centre fuselage tanks	Gal
Nos 1 and 2 tanks, 260 ea	520
Nos 3 and 4 tanks, 220 ea	440
No 5 tank	540
Ventral tank (No 6)	417
Wing integral tanks (Port and Stbd, 450gal each)	900
Wing tip jettison tanks, 2 tanks, 244gal each	488
Total:	3,305

Fuel: Avtag or Kerosine
Engine *oil* capacity — 13.6pt each

In service the PR9 proved its worth over more than 20 years and it was the equipment of the last operational Canberra squadron, No 39, which disbanded at Wyton on 29 May 1982.

During that long period of service it had, oddly enough for a high altitude design, spent much of its operating life in the low-level role, and owing to the security nature of these operations it was little heard of in the aviation world. Nevertheless a climb of 2½min from wheels off to 30,000ft was still remarkable performance for a bomber-size aircraft in 1982 when the Mk 9s were withdrawn from service, and all pilots who served with them held them in very high regard.

Above left:
An operational HA PR9 in the camouflage paint scheme of the 1970s. *MoD via RAF Wyton*

Left:
HA PR9 operational close-up.
MoD via RAF Wyton

Below:
WH793 in its last role, at the Royal Aircraft Establishment modified for upper air gust research on the Concorde programme.
British Aerospace

16 Mk 9 Structural Testing

The flight development of a new type involves a number of key points or test goals which come under the official heading of 'high risk trials'.

In most jet aircraft maximum design speeds are achieved in level flight, often with excess power in hand, and the one-time famous terminal velocity dive to establish its structural integrity at the maximum achievable dive speed has long since become part of aviation and Hollywood history; but among the areas in which major risks can still occur are flight resonance or flutter, stalling and spinning, and structural demonstration at maximum design speed and g. In the first of these, airframes still occasionally encounter 'flutter' or vibratory instability of the structure which can result in failure of wing or tail causing damage to or loss of the aircraft; examples of this occurring with the DC-8 prototype in America in 1960 and with the Mirage F1 in France in 1967.

In the second, super stall or spin recovery problems may be encountered as in the prototype trials of the Hunter, Javelin, F-104, BAC 1-11, Trident and Hansa Jet in recent times.

In the case of structural demonstration the design is put to its most severe test at the combined conditions of maximum speed and weight and the designed maximum g load. Normally the stress calculations have proved right, but it was still possible for some unpredicted factor to occur and lead to trouble.

After testing the Canberra successfully through eight different variants including structural demonstration and then re-proving this case following the loss of a Mk 2 on test by the USAF in America, a totally unexpected problem occurred with the Mk 9.

This very high altitude reconnaissance version with increased wing area and with the big Rolls-Royce Avon RA24 engines similar to those in the Lightning, was considered to be no more than a routine extension of the long line of successful Canberra developments, and after the initial handling tests had gone normally the remaining tests were felt to be routine. The test programme was in the hands of Don Knight as project pilot while Beamont continued with the Lightning which was considered the major test programme at Warton at that time.

The Mk 9 gave no trouble until its final test prior to evaluation by Boscombe Down which was to be the structural demonstration at 5g at design IAS.

After a preliminary check at slightly lower air speed, Knight finally set the Canberra up for this test in smooth air at low level a few miles out to sea off Southport, and steadily pulled on the g in a port turn. At the test point of 5g and just as he was about to roll out of the turn, the aircraft began a violent and uncontrollable roll to starboard into a steep spiral dive and a brilliant orange glare lit up the cockpit. There was no response to lateral control and in seconds as the sea came up the pilot had to eject, his parachute developing just prior to his feet hitting the water. The Canberra hit the sea nearby in a sheet of flame and the observer was killed.

Knight was recovered unhurt and gave a clear and detailed report of the circumstances; and after a difficult operation by the Navy's recovery divers in the muddy waters of Liverpool Bay the wreckage and instrumentation were brought up and the failure pieced together. On the revised wing the leading edge wing-root skin attachments to the fuselage were shown to have failed as the new, larger wing had flexed under extreme load. The skin had peeled back and the wing had failed upwards.

The investigation and necessary redesign came under the direction of Don Crowe, and when the first revised production Mk 9, XH136, reached the flight stage with modified wing skin attachments and was prepared for re-proving the structural demonstration, Beamont took time off from the Lightning to do the trial.

It had been several years since he had been involved in regular Canberra work and the aeroplane was no longer as familiar as before.

The Mk 9, gleaming in its new silver finish, seemed heavy and cumbersome after the Lightning, even though its take-off and climb performance were still remarkable with the big 'Lightning' engines; but after two intermediate sorties to calibrate strain-gauge and wing deflection instrumentation he felt well in tune with the aeroplane again.

On the day, 20 January 1960, the weather was not very helpful as is so often the case with test flying in this country. There was heavy grey cloud cover and a light drizzle was mixed up in industrial smoke, bringing visibility down to about two miles.

The test point was planned for 4,000ft and it was questionable whether there would be sufficient visual reference at that height in these conditions. The test could not easily be carried out on instruments while pulling 140lb load on the stick and controlling speed in a vertically banked turn to within an accuracy of $2\frac{1}{2}$kts and to 5g with no scatter at all, but all concerned were anxious to get the trial over and Beamont decided to have a look at the weather.

On easing the modified production Mk 9 off the runway at about 90% of the total available thrust, full power being unnecessary with these big engines, conditions looked even less suitable. Visibility in the rain and smoke haze was down to about $1\frac{1}{2}$ miles, but at 4,000ft the ground was still in sight and a trial run was set up aiming to pass over the airfield with the River Ribble as a clear landmark just prior to the test point, it being necessary to ensure that this test was carried out overland and not over a heavily populated area.

A run out to the north at 420kts showed that conditions were smooth and non-turbulent and that visibility of the ground below could just be maintained, but it confirmed that there would be virtually no horizon reference in the turn.

Turning southward on to a radar bearing to Warton RPB opened the RA24s to full power and trimmed against the sharp nose-up change of trim. Quickly the runways of Warton appeared below shining in the rain, then the estuary, and already at limiting speed it was time to trim back the engine power. A final selection on the instrumentation panel — a radio call to confirm the test position and direction of turn, and then smoothly into a left turn easing back on the stick until the bank was nearly vertical.

Outside reference was lost in the murk, height checked on the VSI, power increased to compensate as speed dropped off in the turn, and then from $2\frac{1}{2}$g the wheel was pulled back firmly against the rapidly increasing force gradient.

With speed dropping to the exact test point and normal acceleration 4.8-4.9 and then 5g exactly, a final pull to 5.1g covered any reading error.

Easing off the g first while throttling back smoothly the Mk 9 was rolled back to wings-level, and then with sense of direction lost momentarily and nothing recognisable in sight in the gloom and mist except the fields directly below, checked on a steady heading at 010° for base which soon appeared out of the rain ahead.

With the airflow roar of limiting speed down to the quiet of cruising conditions RPB noted fuel conditions and confirmed that the weight and cg had been correct for the test and that the accelerometer maximum-reading needle stood at 5.1g. A short radar line-up, and then in a gentle left turn the runway appeared ahead mistily at about three quarters of a mile and the Canberra touched down gently after an eventful 14 minutes. One more 'corner point' had been achieved.

Below:
Production HA PR9 KH136 with revised nose and cockpit, ready for structural re-testing at Warton on 20 January 1960. *British Aerospace*

17 Interdictor — The B(I) Mk 8

Canberra B(I) Mk 8 Official Description:

Description

This aircraft is a midwing monoplane with engines mounted in the wings and carries a crew of 2. This aircraft is readily convertible to a standard bomber within 24 hours. The nose portion of the fuselage is pressurised with hot/cold control and the upper centre fuselage holds fuel tanks 1, 2 and 3, the lower part being the bomb compartment, enclosed by hydraulically retractable doors which are replaceable with alternative doors and a special gun pack. The tail portion is of a standard pattern with variable incidence tailplane. The wings are fitted with integral fuel tanks and jettisonable tanks are carried on the wing tips. Refuelling of all tanks is by ordinary ground methods.

Engine

Number: Two Rolls-Royce jet propelled engines
Type: Avon Mk 109/RA7
Dry Weight: 2,460lb
Rating: Thrust 7,500lb each engine
Starting: Rolls-Royce turbostarter by cartridge

Operational Equipment

VHF   (ARI 5490)
Gee H   (ARI 5829)
Orange Putter   (ARI 5800)
Radio Altimeter AYF   (ARI 5284)
ILS   (ARI 18011)
Radio Compass, Marconi AD 7092D

Dimensions

Span: 64ft   *Length:* 65ft 6in
Height: 15ft 7in
Sweep back at $\frac{1}{4}c$: 13° 33'
Wing thickness chord:
12% at root
9% at tip
Track: 15ft 9in at main wheels
Wheelbase: (triangular) 14ft fwd of main wheels

Armament

This aircraft has a bombing role similar to that described for B Mk 6

In addition this aircraft after conversion to an Interdictor carries a gun pack in the bomb bay consisting of 4×20mm Hispano guns, 2×1,000lb bombs on the wings and 16×4½" flares

Duration of gun fire=50 seconds

Total fuselage fuel weight=11,280lb

Maximum bomb load=10,000lb. With this load acceleration is slightly reduced

Fuel

Centre fuselage tanks:
No 1 tank   535gal
No 2 tank   325gal
No 3 tank   540gal
Wing integral tanks
Port and Stbd, 450gal, 900gal each
Wing tip jettison tanks; 2 tanks,
244gal each   488gal

Total: 2,788gal

Fuel: Avtag or Kerosine
Engine *oil* capacity — 13.6pt each

Controls

Flaps: Split type — 3 position flaps
Total area: 73sq ft
Dive Brakes: Type: finger spoiler, drag channel section. Hydraulically operated
Area: (inner face of brakes to air stream only) 596.8sq in
Autopilot: Smiths Mk 10
Manually operated controls: Electrically operated for trimming purposes only and electrically operated tailplane
Note: Spring tabs are fitted to control surfaces

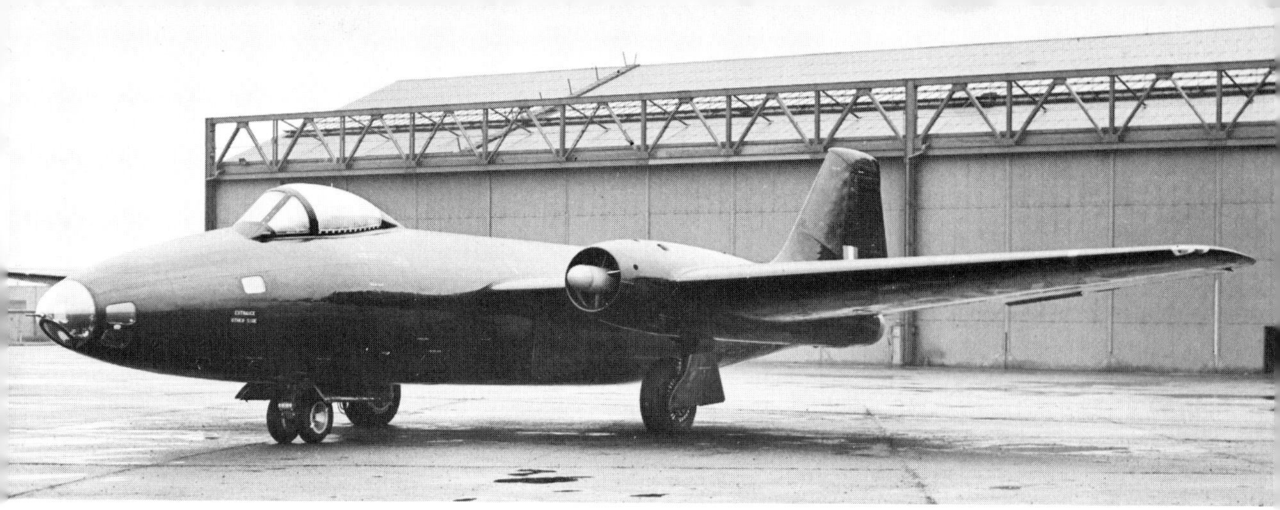

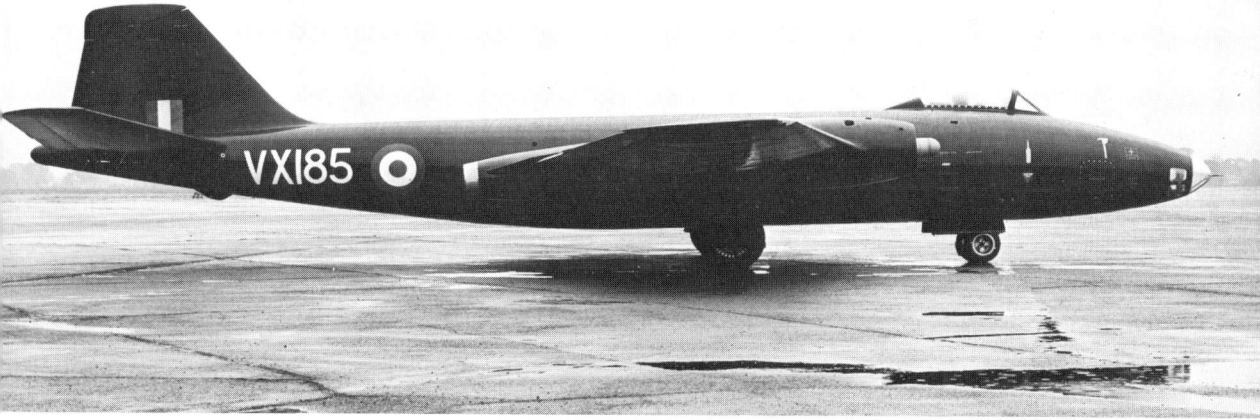

By the early 1950s it had become apparent that already the days of the high altitude unarmed jet bomber were numbered owing to the potential developments in ground-to-air rocket missiles. The Air Staff therefore issued in specification 1B/22D&P a requirement for a specialised interdictor version for low-level operation in visual ground contact armed with a wide range of conventional bombs, rockets and guns. Not mentioned publicly at the time was an alternative nuclear delivery role which became in its service in Nato an important part of the nuclear capability of the Western bloc.

This new Canberra required an entirely new nose fuselage design, and as English Electric had already drained the resources of the north-west and had no spare design capacity at Warton which was by then also heavily involved with the P1 and Lightning, a special design office was set up at Acton in order to tap the potential availability at that time of design staff in the London area.

Top:
VX185, the first B(I)8, converted as a prototype from the B Mk 5 prototype. *British Aerospace via D. Woods*

Above:
VX185 ready for the first flight in the rain on 23 July 1954 at Samlesbury. *British Aerospace*

This bold move was successful and under the management of Albert Draper, a senior Canberra designer from Warton, an entirely new team was formed quickly and work begun on the design and mock-up build of the new variant.

For increased visibility the pilot's station was raised into a fighter-style windscreen and rear-view canopy, and the navigator/bomb-aimer was moved forward of the pilot.

A gunpack with four 20mm Hispano cannon designed by Boulton and Paul Aircraft was fitted into the rear of the bomb bay and fed with the unusually large total of 525 rounds per gun.

Underwing pylons carried either one 1,000lb bomb each or a Matra rocket launcher with 37 Sneb 2in missiles.

To ensure a satisfactory standard for production a prototype was ordered and this was built as a second conversion of the PR3/B5 prototype VX185.

Beamont flew this in its new form from Samlesbury on 23 July 1954, accepting conditions of very heavy rain in order to check as soon as possible visibility through the new curved front windscreen which in the event proved effective in causing the rain to streak away and not interefere too severely with vision.

From the start this variant proved to be another success, and when it was shown in a highly acclaimed public debut at Farnborough in September a significant proportion of its test programme had already been successfully achieved.

The first production Mk 8, WT326, flew at Samlesbury on 8 June 1955, and this series became the basis not only for the main RAF interdictor contribution to Nato for the next seven years but also for the largest export orders for the Canberra including India, New Zealand, Venezuela, South Africa, Rhodesia and Peru.

Below:
Placing the B(I)8 to show the planform.
British Aerospace

Top:
First air photography of the B(I)8, over the Wyre estuary on 28 July 1954. *British Aerospace*

Above:
The B(I)8 on its first flight with the ventral 4 × 20mm gun pack, 28 August 1954; pilot Hillwood. *British Aerospace*

Left:
VX185 comes in for a close-up view of the new canopy and RPB! *British Aerospace*

Top:
First photographic session with the first production B(I)8 along Squire's Gate front on a stormy day, 17 January 1956.
British Aerospace

Above:
WT329 comes in closer.
British Aerospace

Right:
The production B(I)8 shows its gun pack. *British Aerospace*

94

Left:
At Samlesbury some of the production test team in front of a B8 for South Africa — from left to right: Jack Southern, Ron Fox, RPB, Johnny Squier.
British Aerospace

Below:
New equipment for NATO — a newly arrived B(I) Mk 8 for 2nd TAF at Wildenrath in 1956.
MoD via D. Woods

18 Service with the RAF

No 101 was the first Royal Air Force operational squadron to be equipped with the Canberra, Beamont delivering WD936 to RAF Binbrook, Lincolnshire, on 25 May 1951.

Binbrook was commanded by Gp Capt Wally Sheen and 101 Squadron by Wg Cdr Pat Connolly both of whom were great enthusiasts for the new equipment, so that it was no surprise to RPB to be requested by ATC for a 'beat-up' as the Canberra joined the Binbrook circuit.

At light load and in clear weather under a high cloud base the Canberra was put through its aerobatic paces thoroughly for five minutes, keeping within the airfield boundaries almost entirely throughout; and after landing Sheen asked Beamont to talk to the squadron pilots and navigators assembled on the grass outside the squadron offices.

When this was over Sheen said 'there's one more thing before lunch — I am going to fly it!' RPB who had no knowledge of Sheen's current flying ability, pointed out that there was no dual-control in the B Mk 2, and Sheen said 'that's OK, you can come on the jump seat and show me the taps!'

So the first Canberra conversion flight on a Bomber Command Station was carried out in this way without pre-planning or any formal discussion, and that it was completed without incident was a tribute not only to the skill of the station commander but to the simplicity and general ease of control of the Canberra. Nevertheless RPB recalled that he felt he had earned his lunch that day.

So the entry of the Canberra into operational service begun on a high note, but this was slightly subdued two days later by the arrival at Warton of a stern letter from Bomber Command inviting the company to note that on no account in future were Canberra aircraft flown by company pilots to perform aerobatics at RAF stations, as these manoeuvres were 'not suitable' to bomber aircraft.

It appeared that with hindsight the headquarters staff had suddenly become very concerned, and rightly so, at what might happen if their hitherto 'straight-and-level' bomber pilots were let loose on a highly aerobatic aeroplane without proper training and indoctrination. This did in fact eventually

Right:
The first three production B Mk 2s lined up at Warton with Mk 2 prototype VX165 and a Lincoln from RAF Binbrook; early 1951.
British Aerospace

Left:
WD936, the first B Mk 2 for
No 101 Squadron, arrives at
Binbrook. *British Aerospace*

Below:
WD936 by Binbrook control tower,
preparing for the station
commander's flight on 25 May
1951. *British Aerospace*

Left:
R. P. Beamont, Gp Capt Sheen and
Wg Cdr Connolly with WD936 at
Binbrook. *British Aerospace*

Top:
101 Squadron, Binbrook, in late 1951. *Flight*

Above:
101 Squadron Canberras refuelling at Binbrook. *MoD via D. Woods*

Left:
101 Squadron aircrew in 1951. Note WW2 style leather helmets, goggles and Mae Wests. *Flight*

Right:
A Canberra B Mk 2 approaches Binbrook. *MoD via D. Woods*

lead to aerobatic training and in the years to come beautifully-flown Canberra aerobatics by squadron pilots became a feature of air displays throughout the country and abroad, and made a strong contribution to the gathering fame of the aeroplane.

Well before delivery it had become apparent that the Canberra would represent a massive jump for the Bomber Command squadrons which were to exchange their Lincoln and Washington piston-engined bombers for it. In the case of the Lincoln for instance, the Canberra had three crew against seven, almost double the speed, and an additional 20,000ft of altitude. Training was carefully planned, but conversion at Binbrook using Meteor T7 two-seaters initially followed by Meteor F4 single-seaters, proved fairly straightforward with the majority of pilots qualifying on the new bomber after three hours.

Although the first Canberra arrived at 101 in spring 1951, deliveries to the squadron were not completed until December that year due largely to the number of aircraft which were allocated to experimental flying, such as the development of engines and equipment for the high altitudes which the Canberra now made routinely feasible, straight off the production line.

The RAF's first accident with a Canberra occurred when WD895, an early production aircraft collected from Warton by an RAF ferry pilot, and delivered to Hawarden MU on 8 April 1952, was flown the following day by the unit commanding officer, with the ferry pilot as check-pilot in the jump seat.

In landing checks, the check-pilot called for 'All fuel cocks on', and the pilot-under-instruction then switched them all off. In the resulting silence, an attempt was made at an engineless belly-landing on Hooton Park grass airfield nearby, but the Canberra slid off across the boundary, sustaining category 5 damage.

No 231 Operational Conversion Unit was the second RAF unit to receive Canberras. Formed in December 1951 at Bassingbourn, it was to put up the remarkable record of remaining in being with the Canberra for over 30 years. In 1952, deliveries to the Service got into their stride as production geared up at the English Electric factories at Preston and Accrington and the airfield at Samlesbury. No 617 Squadron, also based at Binbrook, received its first Canberra, WD961, as the year opened, and at the end of March a third Binbrook squadron, 12, received its first, WD987.

A Binbrook wing of five Canberra squadrons was completed by the early autumn of 1952, Nos 9 and 50 Squadrons taking their first aircraft on strength in May and August respectively. Also in August 101 became the founder squadron of a second wing forming at Hemswell. By October 1952 the RAF had sufficient Canberras in service, and enough crews who had completed the conversion from piston to jet-power to put up its new aircraft in the annual defence exercise designed to probe the UK air defences. With the remaining Lincolns and Washingtons, Canberras played the part of an attacking force — and their superior perform-

Above:
Air Chief Marshal the Hon Sir Ralph Cochrane, Vice Chief of the Air Staff, and Sqn Ldr John Crampton, No 101 Squadron, 12 October 1952. *MoD via D. Woods*

Below:
An early Canberra formation from Binbrook, 1952. *MoD*

ance in speed and altitude at once showed up wide gaps in the air defence of Great Britain.

The main types with which Fighter Command was equipped at that time — Meteors, Venoms and Sabres — had no chance of intercepting the Canberras at their operating altitude of 45,000ft, and to give the fighters a chance their crews were instructed to come in at 10,000ft below that height — a classic case of fighting with one hand tied behind the back. Even so the intercept record of the defending aircraft was exceptionally poor due to the speed of the 'attacking' Canberras.

Further growth of confidence in the Canberra was demonstrated by the RAF in October 1952 when four aircraft of 12 Squadron, WD987, 990, 993 and 996 — led by Air Marshal Sir Dermot Boyle, took off from Binbrook on what was to be a tour of nearly 25,000 miles through Central and South America on Operation 'Round Trip'. The aircraft were away for almost seven weeks and their tour, during which they gave numerous flying displays which were watched by hundreds of thousands of people in 14 countries, laid the foundation stone for a string of later sales of the Canberra to air forces in South America.

The build-up of the Canberra in RAF service in 1953 was hectic with no fewer than 15 squadrons being established as the output from EE was joined by that from the three sub-contractors, Shorts, A. V. Roe, and Handley Page. Two of the 15 squadrons, Nos 540 and 82 both based at Wyton, received PR3 aircraft, the latter trading what were the last Lancaster bombers. The others were Nos 10, 18, 21, 27 (all at Scampton), 15, 40, 44, 57, 149 (Coningsby), 76 (Wittering), 90 (Marham), 139 (Hemswell) and 192 (Watton). All were bomber squadrons, except 192 which, as a signals command unit, used its aircraft for radio and radar calibration.

There were two occasions during 1953 when the RAF made the world headlines with its powerful new type. The first was immediately after the coronation of the Queen on 2 June when four Canberras flew Operation 'Pony Express' carrying television films of the event to the United States and Canada (48 Canberras were in the RAF coronation royal review fly-past a few weeks later). The second was the England-New Zealand air race of October that year when three of five Canberras entered were from a special RAF flight of No 540 Squadron (the other two were from the Royal Australian Air Force and were

Above:
Leaders of the 1951 South American tour: Sir Dermot Boyle (right) with Sqn Ldr Les Press (centre). *MoD via D. Woods*

Centre right:
B Mk 2 serial WD954, an early production aircraft, was used by Boscombe Down for tropical trials from Khartoum and Nairobi in 1953. It is seen here passing Mount Kilimanjaro, flown by Sqn Ldr Ted Tennant. *MoD*

Bottom right:
Crews of the three Canberra entries for the New Zealand air race in December 1953. Left to right: Wg Cdr Lewis Hodges, Sqn Ldr Currie (Crew 1); Sqn Ldr Les Press (Crew 2); Flt Lt R. L. E. Burton, Flt Lt D. H. Gannon (Crew 3 — the winners); Flt Lt R. Mac A. Furze, Flt Lt T. E. Dunne (Reserves).
Air Historical Branch 6792

the first two B20s to be built there under licence). An RAF PR3 took first place in a total time for the 11,792 miles between London and Christchurch of 23hr 50min for an average speed of 494.5mph; one of the RAAF B20 aircraft was second, and an RAF PR3 was third.

The winning Canberra established point-to-point records London-Basra, and London-Christchurch, and the third RAF Canberra, a PR7, set a point-to-point record London-Colombo.

June 1954 saw the re-equipping with B6s with uprated engines, longer range and higher maximum weight, of 101, the squadron which had introduced the Canberra into the RAF in 1951. No 109 was similarly re-equipped later that year, and in 1955 B6s went to Nos 9, 12, 76, 139 and 617. During 1954, a further 11 RAF squadrons received Canberras for the first time, Nos 35, 115, 207 (Marham), 61, 100 (Wittering), 199 (Honington), 102, 103 (Gutersloh, West Germany), 69 (Laarbruch, West Germany), 58 and 542. All but the last three mentioned received B2s. No 69's Canberras were PR3s and 58 and 542's were PR7s.

Canberras were back in the news in 1954 as a result of a number of overseas tours. These included one to the north of Canada by an aircraft attached to the RAF Flying College, Manby, and named *Aries 1V*, during which it became the first jet aircraft from a British manufacturer to fly in the Arctic, the first flight over the North Pole by a British jet aircraft (also *Airies 1V*) and a visit of 18 Canberras to Sweden.

Then, in February 1955, 101 became the first squadron to take the Canberra to war, flying them on detachment to Singapore against Communist guerillas in what was then called Malaya, now Malaysia. 101 was later joined in these operations by three other Canberra squadrons, Nos 9, 12 and 617.

Canberra squadrons in RAF service peaked at 34 in 1955 with the equipping of three further squadrons in Germany, 104 (Gutersloh) with B2s, 31 (Laarbruch) with PR3s and 80 (Laarbruch) with PR7s.

Reduction of the total number of RAF Canberra squadrons began the following year as Valiant bombers began to arrive in service. Five squadrons, four bomber and one reconnaissance, gave up their Canberras. Three B2 squadrons based in Germany were also disbanded in 1956, but these were replaced by 213 (at Ahlhorn) and 88 (Wildenrath) with interdictor versions of the Canberra, 213 receiving the B(I)6 and 88 the B(I)8. Nos 213

and 88 (and its successor, 14 Squadron) were to operate the interdictors for the next 14 years. The third new Canberra squadron was No 17 (at Wahn) with PR3s. And in May 1956 the RAF established its first Canberra squadron in the Middle East Air Force. This was No 13, based at Akrotiri, Cyprus, with PR7s.

Cyprus, with Malta, rapidly became focal points later that year for a vast concentration of RAF fire power during the Suez affair. Nationalisation by Egypt of the Suez Canal and British and French determination to keep the waterway open freely to international traffic, culminated in October/November 1956 in a massive assault force being assembled in the eastern Mediterranean.

The force included 30 squadrons of RAF aircraft, and 15 of these were Canberra squadrons, all of them except one (No 13, with PR7s, normally based at Akrotiri, Cyprus) on detachment from bases in the UK. Canberra squadrons which took part in the Suez operation were, Nos 9, 10, 12, 13, 15, 18, 27, 35, 44, 57 (57 sent pilots only), 61, 101, 109, 115, 139.

Canberra WH853, of 10 Squadron, dropped the first bombs in the campaign during the night of 31 October on the airfield at Almaza. High level bombing by Canberras and Valiants from 40,000ft was carried out at night because it was known that the Egyptian early-warning radar was unserviceable due to lack of maintenance, and it was considered that the Egyptian Air Force interceptors would be unable to find the intruders under cover of darkness. But attacking under such conditions proved to be a hit-and-miss affair, and three out of seven important Egyptian airfields remained in action, despite being attacked, while two more were partly serviceable.

On the night of 31 October, a large force of Canberras and Valiants was airborne and *en route* for airfield targets, including Cairo West, when the British embassy in Cairo warned that that airfield was at that moment being used by 15 United States transport aircraft to evacuate US citizens. Radio messages via Cyprus to delete Cairo West from the list of targets reached the bomber force just before it entered Egyptian airspace. The action produced its other legends, including the Canberras on a raid which were given a 'fix' on their airfield target by an Egyptian air traffic controller who assumed he was talking to an inbound airliner.

Above:
Interdictors of 2nd ATAF NATO in July 1960. A B(I)8 of 16 Squadron Laarbruch (Wg Cdr V. R. Forsyth) and two

B(I)6s of 213 Squadron, Bruggen (Wg Cdr P. J. Bayley).
Air Historical Branch 19495

Right:
Bombing-up a B Mk 6 at Akrotiri for a sortie in the Suez operation, late 1956. *MoD*

Below:
All five production derivatives of the basic Canberra; from right to left: B2, PR3, T4, B6 and PR7 at Warton outside the Chief Test Pilot's office (previously Petter's) in 1954. *British Aerospace*

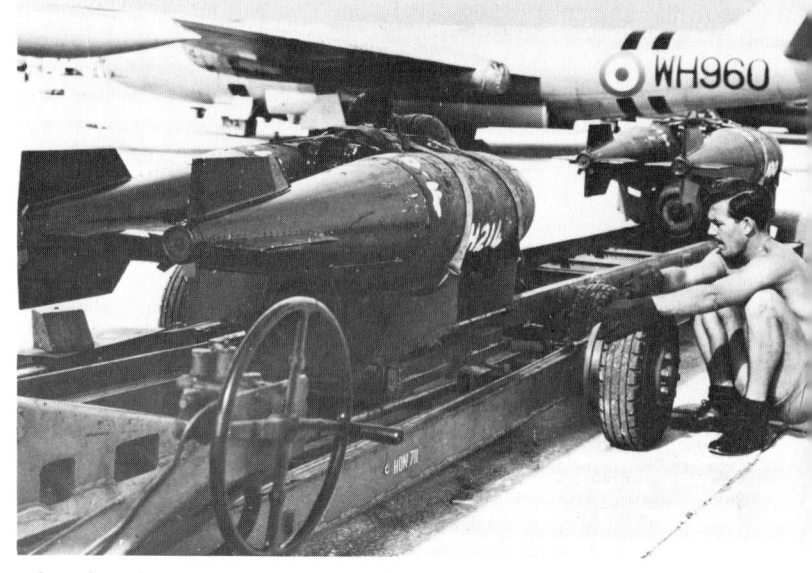

Low-level bombing during the day by a variety of Allied aircraft, including Canberras, produced better result than the night-time strikes, and the PR7s of No 13 Squadron were active on photo-reconnaissance missions. It was on one of these, when the PR7s were despatched over Syria, escorted by French Air Force Thunderflashes, to look for a reported build-up of Soviet aircraft, that the only Canberra (WH799) of the campaign was lost through enemy action — shot down by a Syrian AF MiG-15.

Some months earlier, on the nationalisation by Nasser of the Suez Canal, the crew of an RAF Canberra transiting Egypt on a routine long-range exercise had been taken into custody at gun point after they landed to refuel by euphoric Egyptian soldiers. After a night in the cells the crew, led by Air Cdre Dan Honley (in 1982 with the Society of British Aerospace Companies) pushed open the door to find their guard — and everybody else on the base — sleeping off the previous day's celebrations. Tiptoeing past the recum-

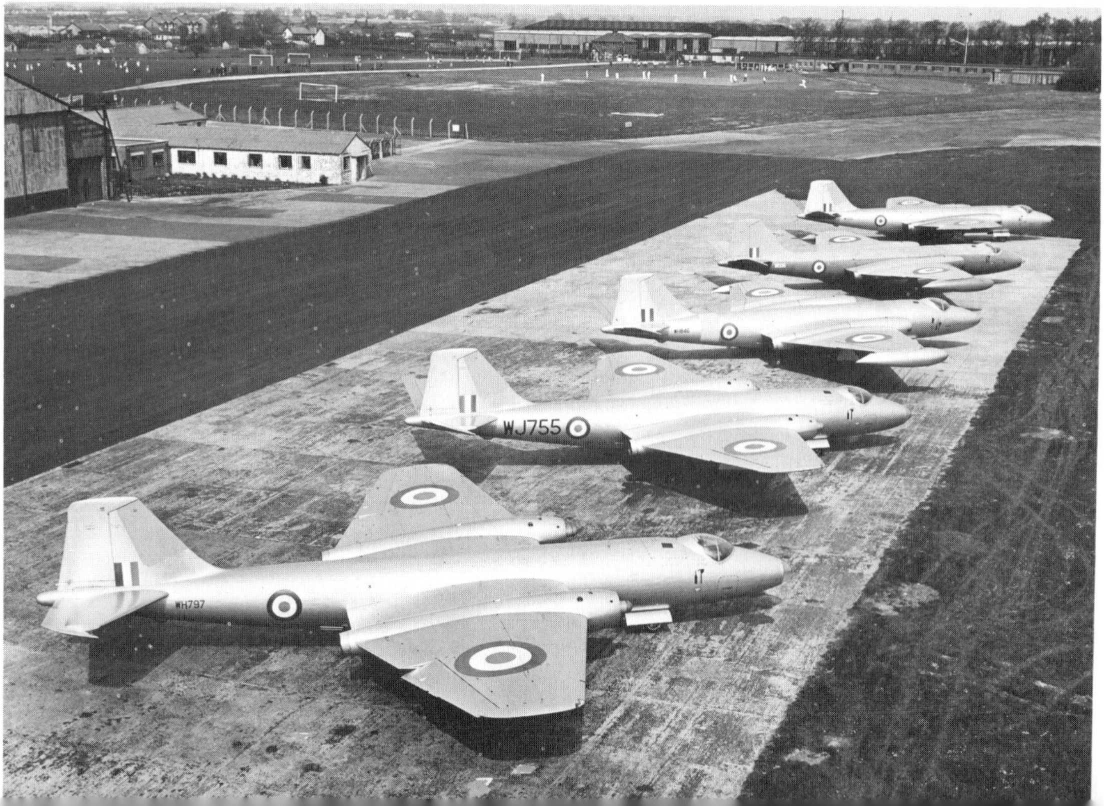

Above:
Samlesbury production in the 1950s: B(I) Mk 8, B6 and T4. *British Aerospace*

bent bodies they retrieved their confiscated possessions, walked out to their Canberra, started up and flew away.

Five days after the start of the Suez action intense pressure was exerted upon the combatants by the United States and the Soviet Union, with the result that a ceasefire was arranged on 6 November and United Nations forces moved in. Canberras went home, although it was January the following year before the last squadron touched down at its UK base after a brief adventure during which the aircraft had shown up well, albeit against poor opposition.

Ten RAF Canberra squadrons based in Britain were disbanded during 1957, seven of them re-forming at a later stage with aircraft of the new V-bomber force, either Vulcans, Victors or Valiants. But at the same time four new Canberra squadrons flying B2s were being formed in the Middle East, and a fifth, also with B2s, in the Far East at Tengah, Singapore. This was No 45 Squadron and for the next three years it took part in operations against the Communist guerrillas. No 59 Squadron based in Germany received B(I)8s in exchange for its B2s. This whole period of the Canberra in RAF service was marked by a series of long-range training flights under the code-name 'Lone Ranger'.

By the end of 1958 there were 24 Canberra squadrons in the RAF. Nos 61 and 199 Bomber Command squadrons were disbanded, as was 542 (reconnaissance), but 245 was established at Tangmere in Signals Command, with B2s. No 16 Squadron re-formed at Laarbruch with B(I)8s, and No 69, operating PR3s from the same base in Germany was re-numbered 39 and trans-

ferred to Malta. The balance of the Canberra force was now moving away from Britain so that there were more squadrons based abroad than in the UK.

Canberras took on a nuclear role during 1957/58 when the bomber and interdictor versions were gradually withdrawn from service for modifications to enable them to carry atomic weapons and to deliver them by 'tossing' them at the target using the LABS — low altitude bombing system. No 9 Squadron aircraft were the first to be modified.

The last Canberra to be built for the RAF by English Electric, B(I)8 XM936, was delivered in April 1959, but as it arrived three further Canberra bomber squadrons were being disbanded in Britain reducing the UK-based force to four. At the end of 1959 the RAF had 21 Canberra squadrons on strength, including one new one formed during the year. This was No 228 OCU based at Leeming, Yorkshire, with the role of operating T11s to instruct aircrews destined to fly Javelins in radar interception.

Shorts produced the very last new Canberra, PR9 XH177, delivering it at the end of 1960, a year during which this version replaced the PR7s operated by 58 Squadron RAF from Wyton. Also during 1960, No 76 Squadron with B6s was disbanded. The last three Canberra bomber squadrons based in the UK were stood down in 1961, the final squadron being No 35, by which time the Canberra had been in service with the RAF in this role for 10 years. Most of the B6s taken out of service at this time were uprated to either B15 or B16 tactical strike versions, and 32 Squadron in Cyprus became the first to re-equip. No 81 Squadron was formed with PR7s in 1961 at Tengah, so that by the end of that year the RAF Canberra squadron strength was 18 — three in the UK, seven in Germany, six in the Middle East Air Force, and two in the Far East.

No 13 Squadron, at Akrotiri, re-equipped with PR9s in early 1962. Later that year three more squadrons at the same base, Nos 6, 73 and 249, re-equpped with B15s and B16s. No 45 in Singapore also received B15s. B15s were modified during 1962 at Samlesbury to carry the Nord AS30 solid-propellant air-to-ground missile. Also in 1962, aircraft of No 75 Squadron RAF were active against a revolt in Brunei.

PR9s operated in the UK by 58 Squadron were handed over in early 1963 to 39 Squadron in Malta which operated the version alongside 13 Squadron as the eyes of the strike wing of Canberras based in Cyprus. 58 was re-equipped with PR7s. Also in 1963, the RAF's Target Facilities Squadron formed within Fighter Command to provide targets and to carry out dummy attacks, was designated No 85. In 1964, RAF Canberras flew against Indonesia paratroops dropped in Malaysia.

Just as it appeared that the service days within the RAF were numbered, the aircraft gained a new lease of life with the political cancellation by the Labour Government in April 1965 of the TSR2 bomber project, rapidly followed by the political collapse of the Anglo-French VG (variable geometry) bomber project and then the cancellation of

Above:
A TT18 with Rushton targets.
British Aerospace

Right:
Streaming a Rushton target at the beginning of its 20,000ft of cable; 100 Squadron, Wyton.
Flight Refuelling Ltd via D. Woods

Top right:
The pilot's cockpit of a TT18 with the bomb aimer's couch right-centre. *British Aerospace*

the purchase from the United States of the theoretical TSR2 replacement, the General Dynamics F-111. Canberras thus remained the RAF's main tactical strike aircraft until the end of the decade by which time ex-Royal Navy Buccaneers, and F-4 Phantoms heavily Anglicised at great additional cost with Rolls-Royce Speys and UK avionics fits, began to enter service.

No 85 Squadron mentioned above had its T11s converted to 19s with radar removed and uprated ejector seats during 1967/68, and the first T17 designed to give training in ECM (electronic counter-measures) went to 360 Squadron at Watton, late in 1966. Deliveries continued until early 1968 by which time some 20 of this specialised version were in service.

At the close of 1968 the RAF had 20 Canberra squadrons on its strength, 15 of them based abroad. By then it had been in service for 18 years, but there were still more of them in Service than any other aircraft type. As

Britain began to withdraw from her overseas bases and as Buccaneers and Phantoms geared up, Canberra units began to wind down seriously in the late 1960s/early 1970s. No 45 Squadron in Singapore was disbanded in late 1968, as was the Cyprus-based Canberra strike wing consisting of Nos 6, 32, 73 and 294, early the following year. Nos 17, 80 and 213 Squadrons, based in Germany, went in 1969. In the same year 56 Squadron took on strength two Canberras, a B2 and a T4, at its base at Akrotiri to provide interception practice for its BAC Lightning fighters.

But it was not all traffic through the door marked 'exit' for the Canberra, for in early 1970 no less than 21 years after the type had first entered service, a new RAF squadron was formed — No 7, based at St Mawgan, Cornwall. No 7 was equipped with TT18 target tugs equipped with the Rushton system developed by Flight Refuelling Ltd and carried on pylons under each wing, which enabled the high-speed target to be streamed as far as 10 miles behind the aircraft. The Royal Navy had actually been the first to receive TT18s at its Fleet Requirements Unit, Hurn, Hampshire, where they were to replace Meteor target tugs which by this time were getting extremely long in the tooth.

At the end of 1971 the RAF had nine Canberra units. Five were based in the UK on special duties, two were equipped with PR9s — No 13 in Malta and No 39 at Wyton — and two with B(I)8s, Nos 3 and 16, both still in Germany. During that same year a few PR7s were converted into T22s with radar equipment in extended noses for operation by the RN Fleet Requirements Unit, Yeovilton, Somerset. B(I)8 interdictors were finally retired from RAF service in early 1972 when 3 Squadron exchanged them for Harriers and 16 Squadron for Buccaneers, so leaving the PR9s of 13 and 39 Squadrons as the only Canberras in front-line service. But while this withdrawal process was going on, 85 Squadron, providing target facilities, was growing to the extent that its 25 aircraft — B2s, T4s and T19s — were split into two Squadrons numbered 85 and 100, 100 having been a B2 squadron up to the middle of 1959.

Canberras now performed second-line duties in six squadrons based in the UK, apart from the two squadrons engaged on photo-reconnaissance. The six were Nos 85 and 100, mentioned immediately above, 7 using TT18s to tow targets, 51 and 98 using B6s and E15s on signals and calibration duties, and 360 with T17s training ECM operators.

Right:

Flaunting its tailplane insignia of a skull and crossbones is a Canberra of 100 Squadron at RAF Marham, Norfolk, being prepared for another gunnery practice sortie for Lightnings and Phantoms over the North Sea or the Bristol Channel. Airmen are straightening out the target banner which will be hooked up from the runway as the aircraft takes off and then towed at the end of 900ft of nylon cable. The 'peppered' banner will later be dropped off at the fighter base concerned with the day's 'shoot'.
Peter Stevenson MoD

Having peaked at 34 squadrons in Royal Air Force service in 1955, Canberras had reduced to the equivalent of three and a half squadrons by the latter half of 1982, but this remarkable aircraft was earmarked for RAF service for a further 10 years after that and informed opinion was that their life was likely to be extended still further so that some might well be still in service at the turn of the new century.

RAF Wyton near Huntingdon became the 'home' of the remaining RAF Canberras, and here were gathered a total of around 40 aircraft of several marks with Nos 100 and 360 Squadrons, an operational conversion unit — the famous 231 OCU which formed in March 1947 and which trained Canberra crews right through from December 1951 — No 1 Photographic Reconnaissance Unit, the 'rump' of No 39 Squadron. All of the aircraft had a

Above:

An E15 of 100 Squadron landing at Coltishall in 1982. Note typical flat landing attitude due to low wing-loading and unswept wings. WH583 was built as a B Mk 6 by Avro and served with 101 Squadron at Suez in 1956 and with 9 Squadron in Cyprus before conversion to E15 by Marshall's of Cambridge. *MoD*

fairly low state of readiness war role under Nato.

No 360 was a most unusual squadron in that it was joint RAF-Royal Navy, and during our visit to Wyton during the summer of 1982 had an RN commander as commanding officer. The break-down was 75% RAF and 25% RN, which meant that COs, carrying out two-year spells of command, were RAF for three spells in succession, and then RN for one spell. Personnel were mixed in the same proportions on a permanent basis, from pilots and navigators (called observers if RN),

Above:
A T17 — the highly specialised version of the B Mk 2 used for sophisticated electronic countermeasures training — of 360 Squadron, Wyton. *British Aerospace*

Left:
A close-up of the nose fairings of the T17.
MoD via Wyton

Below left:
This shows the effect of T17 jamming on a radar screen.
MoD via Wyton

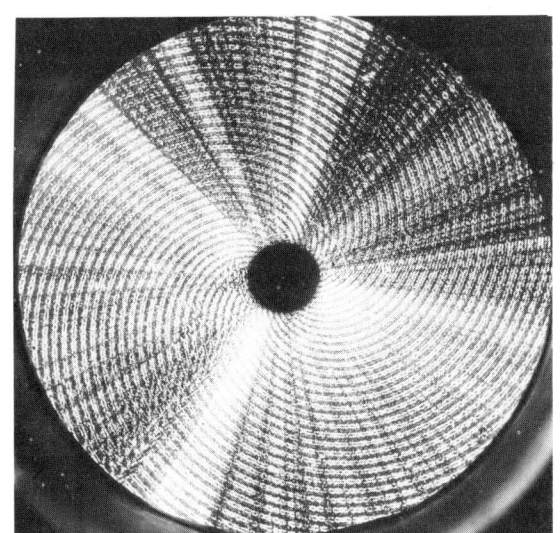

through engineers, to adminstrators. Jobs were carried out as if in one single Service, so that Canberras flown by, say, an RAF pilot and an RN observer were common, the only distinction being in the uniforms and a certain amount of inter-Service crew-room banter.

The squadron badge and motto of No 360 gave its role away. The badge pictures *Melese Laodamia Druce* which, for the uninitiated, is a moth which has the remarkable ability to receive a bat's echo-locating signals, propagate spurious signals in return, and thereby throw the bat's target-acquisition system into confusion. The moth rests on Neptune's trident, indicating the joint RAF-RN nature of the squadron. The motto is *Confundemus*, or 'We shall throw into confusion' — which gives a further clue.

No 360's role, was in fact, ECM — electronic countermeasures training. It operated T17s with the long nose covered in bumps containing a variety of aerials ('ugly' according to outside observers, 'distinguished' according to squadron members). The squadron was born on 1 April, a propitious date for aspiring 'spoofers', 1966, from a marriage of No 831 Naval Air Squadron and No 97 Squadron RAF, at RAF Watton, and was in 1982 the largest squadron of land-based aircraft within the Nato European area providing regular ECM training for users of military electronic sensors and communications equipment.

The T17 was a conversion of the B2 Canberra, with its bomb bay containing a comprehensive range of jamming equipment which derived electrical supplies from two engine-driven turbo-alternators. Each aircraft had a crew of three — pilot, navigator, and air electronics officer (named the electronic warfare officer) who was responsible for the management of the ECM systems and who sat at a console discrete to the T17 on the right-hand side of the rear compartment.

The 360 Squadron T17s, their equipment 'tweaked' to produce high performance, and to represent the Warsaw Pact electronic warfare threat, exercised with air-defence elements of all three Services, basically attempting to confuse the air-defence radars, whether those for early warning or the airborne intercept AIs on board the Lightning, Phantom and ADV Tornado, or land-based and shipborne fire-control and airborne early warning radars. Aircraft availability was high, particularly considering the large amounts of complicated equipment carried.

The T17s also made the life of the 'opposition' frustrating by scattering chaff, known as 'window' in World War 2, from wingtip pods, and by 'spoofing' over the radio telephone — recording RT chatter between controller and fighters in an exercise and re-broadcasting the tape a few nights later during a further exercise was a favourite game.

According to the squadron, their prowess in throwing into confusion well-planned exercises resulted in them being held in awe by their 'customers', while the electronic warfare officer was viewed in some quarters as a wizard endowed with mystical powers, who flew wearing a big black hat — an impossible physical feat as anybody who has ever squirmed his way into the rear compartment of a T17 will appreciate. The squadron denied a rumour that it arranged for the surveillance radar in Cyprus to be struck by lightning while it was flying there, and also stated that its ability to reduce RT to the level of a Mad Hatter's tea party did not mean that its in-flight rations were laced with rum.

In all, each T17 was equipped with some 20 aerials. No 360 Squadron was 90% engaged in ECM training, but it also carried out some consultancy services for the aerospace industry.

In 1982 No 100 Squadron's role at Wyton was target facilities duties and for this it used a mixed bag of Canberra B2s, PR7s, E15s and TT18s. It moved to Wyton in January 1982 and, having absorbed crews and aircraft from Nos 7, 13, 85 and 98, became one of the largest squadrons in the RAF. No 100 was originally formed as the RFC's first specialised night bomber squadron in February 1917. It has had a lengthy association with the Canberra having been among the first to take the then new aircraft on its strength in 1954. On 1 September 1959, the squadron was disbanded.

In May 1962, 100 was re-formed with Victor B2s, but with the passing of the nuclear deterrent role to the Royal Navy the squadron was again disbanded in September 1968. But then in February 1972 it was re-formed once more, this time with Canberra B2s and T19s for target facilities duties. Its B2s were basically the original bomber aircraft; its E15s a version with an avionics update of the B15 which itself was a development of the B6 for the tactical nuclear bombing role based in Cyprus, and with more powerful Avon 109 engines; its PR7s were the photographic version of the B6 with a slightly longer fuselage; and its TT18s were the adaptation of the B2 which was carried out in the late 1960s for the towing of the Rushton and sleeve targets. The main difference from the B2 was that the TT18 had twin attachment points under its wings, and an electrical control panel. It had a novel minor modification — rear-view mirrors inside the navigator's window in the left-hand side of the fuselage and inside a small window cut into the right-hand side of the fuselage through which the behaviour of the underwing winches could be monitored.

All the types of Canberras flown by No 100 acted as air-to-air 'silent' targets for fighters and ground-to-air and sea-to-air defence systems — that is, targets on to which the defenders could 'home' without actually firing their weapons. They frequently took part in exercises for the training of fighter controllers, and worked with the T17s of No 360, their fellow Wyton Canberra squadron, in simulating enemy attacks on the UK. In spite of its age, the Canberra's agile performance provided the defenders with a realistic target which was able to give them a hard time, particularly in bad weather conditions. E15s were also used for flight-checking and calibration of radars and navigation aids. The TT18 was the only Canberra type which took part in 'live' target practice, due to its ability to stream the Rushton flyable target on the end of 20,000ft of cable. This provided practice for Rapier batteries, and sleeve targets streamed in similar fashion provided practice for naval gunnery.

No 1 Photographic Reconnaissance Unit at Wyton was particularly proud of their Canberras, the PR9 — the last major new mark of the aircraft built, with bigger engines (Avon 200s, without reheat, 11,250lb of thrust), and bigger wings in both span and chord. 'Built like a battleship and the GT version of all the Canberras', the squadron said. The PR9 was initiated originally as Britain's contribution to what was to be President Eisenhower's 'open skies' policy, a form of international *detente* under which East and West would have been allowed to make PR sorties over each other's territory — a plan which came to nothing. It was the only version which did not employ cartridge starting, using a iso-propylnitrate (IPN) chemical starter instead. The pilot climbed a ladder up the side of the fuselage to the cockpit, and the navigator/camera operator sat in a seat in the nose of the aircraft which swung open to allow him in an out, and viewed the outside world through a downward facing periscope.

The navigator had an ejector seat, and was blown through a frangible panel in the top of the aircraft nose in emergency. Each aircraft carried nine cameras, and while the front part of the bomb bay carried an extra fuel tank, the rear part carried flares. On the PR9, the bomb bay was thus renamed the flare bay. The title No 1 PRU was afforded the half squadron of PR9s which remained at Wyton in June 1982 on the stand-down of No 39 Squadron. It had nostalgic connotations as the original photographic reconnaissance unit, formed in 1939, had the same title. The Wyton PR9s, which in the summer of 1982 still bore the 39 Squadron insignia on their tails, were the last of what, at the peak, was a major force of PR Canberras — 11 squadrons in all. Their task in 1982 was high and medium-level PR and survey at up to 50,000ft, and an important part of their work was vertical photography for updating of Ordnance Survey maps.

No 231 OCU operated in 1982 seven T4 trainers, one B2, and one B2(T) one of three B2s which were equipped with a more sophisticated navigation fit including Green Satin doppler and twin VOR, to full airways standard. The main role of the unit, which moved to Wyton in July 1982, was to train crews, usually first tourists, on to the Canberra. Six courses a year were undertaken, with a maximum of six students in each course.

Although only a small unit in 1982, 231 held the twin records of the longest-serving OCU in the RAF, and the longest-serving jet

Left:
Precision formation in T4s by instructors of 231 OCU — at one time the only bomber formation aerobatic team in the world.
MoD via RAF Wyton

Below :
The badge of No 231 OCU.
MoD via RAF Wyton

conversion unit in the world. As indicated above, 231 was formed on 15 March 1947, with Mosquitos, and after standing down in December 1949 on the withdrawal of that aircraft type as a bomber from the RAF, re-formed on 1 December 1951, at Bassingbourn, Cambridgeshire, with the task of training aircrew on the Canberra. It received its first Canberras in February 1952, its instructors having trained up for the jet role on Meteor T7s and PR10s, and the first Canberra course which was to take the RAF out of the era of the 'heavies' and into the jet bomber era making a quantum jump overnight in speed, altitude and range, began on 27 May that year.

Up to the time of writing in the autumn of 1982, the OCU, over 30 years, had trained the remarkable number of over 7,000 aircrew on the Canberra from the RAF, the Royal Navy, Commonwealth and foreign air forces. 231 kept pace with the many and varied roles which were devised for the Canberra over the years. The unit began with the B2, and by June 1953 had 26 of this version on its strength. In November that year it received the first of seven PR3s, and a photographic reconnaissance training unit, 237(PR)OCU, was in fact split off from 231 and established at RAF Merryfield and then RAF Wyton until disbanding in January 1958, when the role was returned to 231 at Bassingbourn.

But 231 had more than just the passive training role. After showing its prowess with T4s in a major UK air defence exercise in the spring of 1956, Bassingbourn was given a wartime task similar to that of operatonal Canberra squadrons and was expected to supply aircraft in support of SACEUR. As a result of a request in 1960 from overseas commands, 231 introduced low-level training with the PR Canberras — down to 250ft dual and 1,000ft solo — and a request for a similar form of training for the strike element followed. A new syllabus incorporating the necessary changes was drawn up and put into effect in the early summer of 1961. A further specialist training task given the unit during that period was instruction in LABS technique, the delivery by Canberras of nuclear weapons. The main versions of the Canberra used by 231 throughout were T4s for pilot conversion and crew familiarisation, and B2s and PR3s for specialist training.

Uniforms of many types and shades were seen at 231 over the years, reflecting the diversity of uses to which the Canberra has been put. RN officers attended a course in the autumn of 1966 prior to joining the Joint Service special-purpose Canberra squadrons at Watton; while a variety of air force officers from South American countries were trained, as were those from the Ethiopian Air Force. German civilians employed by the West German Ministry of Defence to fly their Canberras were also trained at Bassingbourn, as were a wide range of RAF officers from junior officers freshly out of training school, through wing commanders on their way to take over squadrons, to the most august pupil of all, the then Chief of the Air Staff, Sir Dermot Boyle, who 'refreshed' in October 1958, on a Bassingbourn T4. An interesting experiment in 'civilianisation' took place at the OCU during the 1960s when aircraft servicing and allied support services were taken over, as an economy measure, by Airwork. Contracting out to civilian firms had been tried previously with success in Flying Training Command, but this was its first test in an operational command. The scheme worked well, with the aircraft maintained to a high standard. There were savings for the taxpayers in that because there were no postings there was less interference with unit routines, while the economic 'deadweight' of camp families and the administrative 'tail' were missing.

Perhaps one of the most abiding memories of the thousands of men who passed through Bassingbourn and crewed the Canberra is of the extremes of body heat and cold that the aircraft could generate. For pilots the Canberra bubble canopy could be a greenhouse, magnifying the sun until, after a long grind of 'circuits and bumps', flying suits would literally turn black with perspiration and recourse had to be made to what were known as the 'pit-head baths' at the OCU for a complete change of clothing. Conversely, on long high-altitude flights, crew members in the navigator's compartment behind the pilot would be badly affected by chill creeping through the aircraft skin, so much so, that even if several layers of clothing were worn, the cold brought severe discomfort, and crews were known to pummel each other in an effort to bring a semblance of life back to their circulation.

Over three decades the quality of training provided by 231 OCU ensured that the name Bassingbourn became synonymous with the name Canberra; and much credit for the successful introduction of the Canberra into service with the RAF and many overseas air forces was due to the dedicated skill and professionalism of all ranks of 231 in setting and sustaining the highest standards of conversion training for the era of the jet bomber.

19 A Best Seller Abroad

Australia

The United States (see chapter 11) and Australia were the first two overseas customers for the Canberra and the only two to establish their own production under licence from English Electric in the UK. Australian interest in the Canberra showed itself as early as 1949, concurrently with that evinced by the Americans, but it was not until 1951 that firm plans were promulgated for the building of the B20 version — essentially the B2 with integral wing fuel tanks — at Government Aircraft Factory's works at Fisherman's Bend, Melbourne. A total of 48 B20s were eventually produced from parts manufactured at GAF, with final assembly and flight test following at the factory and airfield at Avalon. Commonwealth Aircraft Corporation produced RA7 Avons for the final 20 Australian Canberras.

But before all this, a hitch occurred during the early evaluations which could have had far-reaching implications.

In 1950 the RAAF sent a technical mission to Warton to evaluate the first prototype VN799 including a Service test pilot, and the latter on his first sortie encountered a major engine problem.

Following a simulated single-engine approach the aircraft was seen to initiate a go-around to the accompaniment of the unmistakable sound of an engine 'surge' (compressor stall).

After climbing flatly away 799 reappeared overhead, still 'surging' and now with a brilliant ball of fire under the port engine nacelle.

An urgent radio instruction to shut down the port engine with the HP and LP (high and low pressure) cocks resulted in the visible flames extinguishing, and the prototype was then carefully brought round to a single-engine landing, trailing smoke all the way.

The fire vehicles put out any residual fire, and then the extent of the damage was seen to be massive.

Below:
Handover in July 1951 of first 'pattern' aircraft for Australia — A84.307 — with RAF personnel and (left to right): unknown, unknown, Hollock, Ellison, Shorrock, Pickthall, Wg Cdr Cumming RAAF, Flt Lt Harvey RAAF, Air Cdre Strang-Graham, RPB, Sarginson, unknown, unknown. *British Aerospace*

It was a characteristic of the axial Avons that a compressor stall would normally not produce a dramatic indication to the pilot but only a roughness sensation coupled with unmistakable thrust loss, and if persisted with as in this case an eventual fire-warning light.

It seemed that in the unfamiliar environment of a new type the pilot had not recognised the symptoms from his briefing and had failed to take the vital immediate action of throttling back the engine out of surge. In the circumstances it was a fortunate outcome because another half-minute of full-throttle 'surge' fire would most probably have burnt through the main spar.

As it was the damage was repaired and VN799 returned to the test programme in less than a month. The Australians were not deterred by their experience which at least confirmed for them the single-engine capability of the Canberra.

To start up Australian production, two B2s built by English Electric were bought as patterns. Numbered WD939 and WD983 they were destined for the RAF in the first Canberra contract but were 'short-circuited' to Australia where they were given the serial numbers A84-307 and A84-125. The former was flown out to Darwin in August 1951 by an Australian crew in 21½ hours' flying time for the 10,240 miles over four days, breaking several unofficial records and becoming the first jet aircraft to fly between England and Australia. A84-125 was flown out the following year, and was followed by two more Canberras under a loan agreement.

GAF's first B20, numbered A84-201, made its maiden flight from Avalon on 29 May 1953, and it was delivered for trials to the Royal Australian Air Force a few weeks later. As mentioned in the chapter on Canberras in RAF service, the RAAF entered the first two B20s built by GAF in the 1953 London-New Zealand air race, and one of them came second. The RAAF formed their first two Canberra squadrons in 1955: Nos 2 and 6 based at Amberley receiving B20s in exchange for the Lincoln bombers which they had been operating up to then. No 1 Squadron RAAF became a Canberra squadron in July 1958, and in December that year GAF completed its order for 48 B20s, the final 20 of which had Avon RA7 engines produced in Australia. GAF then produced seven T4-type trainers, designated T21s, by modifications to five of their own B20s, and two B2s which had been sent to the UK.

One squadron of the Royal Australian Air Force, No 2, flew Canberras alongside USAF B-57s in Vietnam, serving for four years from 1967 to 1971 during which they carried out 11,963 missions for the loss of two aircraft and one crew.

No 2 Squadron's eight Canberras began their service in Vietnam bombing from 20,000ft at night under ground radar direction, but soon began taking part in low-level visual strikes under the command of USAF forward air controllers. Their first came loss in November 1970 when a Canberra disappeared without a trace after a bombing mission at 22,000ft; the second in March the following year when an aircraft was hit by a surface-to-air missile, the crew ejecting safely. No 2 Squadron flew its final Vietnam operation in May 1971, and then ferried back to Australia to specialise in reconnaissance and target-towing.

Nos 1 and 6 Squadrons RAAF had their Canberras replaced in 1971 with F-4E Phantoms, but 2 Squadron flew on with its B20s for a further 10 or more years, and No 1 OCU continued operating B20s and T21s.

The RAAF eventually retired its Canberras on 26 June 1982, bringing the date forward from 1984, as planned, because of increasing maintenance costs. At the end, the Service had nine aircraft left, eight with 2 Squadron, at Amberley, and one with the Aircraft Research and Development Unit, at RAAF Edinburgh, South Australia. No 2 Squadron Canberras, used for photo-reconnaissance, aerial survey work and target towing, were to be replaced by a civil twin-jet executive aircraft type.

Venezuela

The first straight sale to a foreign customer (as opposed to overseas licence agreements) came in January 1953 to Venezuela which ordered six B2s. EE had in fact been so confident of the order that it had started work on the aircraft in the closing months of 1952 as they came down the line under Ministry of Supply contracts. This procedure of 'diverting' aircraft due to go to the RAF to foreign buyers in order to assure the early delivery which many of the purchasers demanded, and which had the effect of beating off any foreign competition for the orders, was often followed in subsequent contracts.

The first aircraft delivered to the Fuerzas Aereas Venezolonas was B Mk 2 serial number 1-A39 which arrived at the FAV main base at Maracay, Boca de Rio, on 1 April 1953 flown out by an RAF crew.

Above:
The first B Mk 2 for Venezuela taking off from Samlesbury, March 1953. The aircraft demonstrated for President Jimenez on 5 April.
British Aerospace via D. Woods

Beamont was in charge of the handover party and at the invitation of the FAV flew a demonstration at the base that afternoon. It was soon apparent that this had created something of a sensation and the following day a request was received by the British Air Attaché Wg Cdr Hackforth for the Canberra to be demonstrated before the President, Perez Jimenez, on the following Monday morning at 8.30am at La Calorta, a small airfield near the centre of the capital, Caracas. Then the problems began.

It was late on Friday and the weekend was a religious holiday, so that it was soon apparent that no assistance could be expected on the Saturday or Sunday in preparing the aircraft at Maracay for the essential 60-mile positioning flight to Caracas.

Nothing daunted, HM Air Attaché flew Beamont in his official Devon aircraft to Maracay on the Saturday morning, with a party consisting of the English Electric technical representative and those of Rolls-Royce and de Havilland (the latter had no commitment but came to give a hand in any case).

At Maracay the worst fears were realised. There were no hangar staff, the Canberra was at the back of its hangar and parked squarely in front of it was a B-25 Mitchell on jacks and apparently left in this position by its American military mission supervisors for reasons which could only be surmised at, but it was well known that the Canberra deal had been very strongly opposed throughout by the Americans.

So in blazing tropical heat the British party set about opening the hangar, taking the B-25 down off jacks and manhandling it out of the way, all without authorisation, and then pushing out and pre-flighting the Canberra.

By late afternoon all was ready but then a major problem appeared. Despite all efforts it had not been possible to obtain engine-starter cartridges from the contract supply which had been located in bonded customs store at the Port of Maracay. This would not be open until after the holiday, and the only cartridges left after the delivery and demonstration flights were two for each engine. This would give engine starts for the flight to Caracas and one chance only for the President's demonstration on Monday. Then if that was successful the aircraft would either have to stay at Caracas until more cartridges could be found or it would have to fly back to Maracay without landing at la Calorta.

With these narrow options Beamont flew 1-A39 with the English Electric rep as passenger over the mountains to land on the rough airfield of La Calorta with the sun well down behind the high mountain ridge bordering one side of the field, and he noted that the demonstration next day would be restricted by the mountain on one side and the city of Caracas on the other.

Monday 6 April brought a new surprise — the unrelenting sunshine of the previous weeks had given way to dark cloud cover and visibility in mist of about one mile. The close-by mountains were out of sight, but the local experts suggested that the sun would soon burn this cloud off.

At 8.15 on the misty airfield some light patches began to appear in the cloud overhead and with about two miles visibility it was decided that the flight would be 'on', and

115

Above:
The third Venezuelan at Warton before delivery, 1953.
British Aerospace

that after explanation to the President the aircraft would fly back to Maracay afterwards.

Promptly at 8.30 the entourage appeared and the President was shown round the Canberra; and signifying that he was ready to see it fly he shook hands with Beamont who then started the engines on the last two cartridges.

A radio call to the tower produced no response so the Canberra began to taxi and at this point a C-47 appeared through the mist on final approach. This landed and then before the Canberra could line up another C-47 appeared out of the haze, and then another.

Calling the tower again produced a distorted message confirming that these were an unspecified number of 'troop carriers' landing and that the Canberra was 'on its own responsibility'.

There had been no briefing on this and only assurances that there would be 'no other traffic during the President's demonstration'; so Beamont decided that this was likely to be another manifestation of American mission activity and that as the President was waiting he should not be kept waiting any longer.

The Canberra was quickly airborne at light load and turning tightly round the airfield found another C-47 on the approach to land. This was to be the pattern of the display which had to be carried out between, over and sometimes under a continued stream of Dakotas.

The now broken cloud base remained limiting also, but seeing the foot of the mountain beginning to appear the Canberra made its final pass low across the field towards the spectators before pulling up to disappear in cloud apparently directly towards the mountain en route for Boca de Rio.

This was all well received by the authorities and the Canberra began its Venezuelan service with a high reputation not only at the first jet bomber in South America, but as a very agile one.

The remaining four aircraft for Venezuela were delivered by civilian crews from Silver City Airways, and one of these consisting of J. W. Hackett, pilot, and P. J. Moneypenny, navigator, was to be involved in many long-range flights with Canberras as the years went by.

Those early delivery days were recalled by Johnny Hackett, who after two years on detachment from Silver City Airways joined English Electric, later taking part in the development-flying programmes of the BAC 1-11, VC10 and Concorde. He was, in 1982, flight operations manager of British Island Airways, based at Gatwick airport.

Hackett had flown Meteors in the RAF, but with Peter Moneypenny, his navigator, and a second Silver City crew, Barry Damon, pilot, and Mac McLaughlan, navigator, was sent by Silver City to Driffield to refresh on Meteors, and then to Bassingbourn OCU where they had their first experience on Canberras. His first delivery flight, with Peter Moneypenny, was the second aircraft for Venezuela routeing via Gander, Friendship airport Baltimore, Jamaica and then Venezuela. This was in 1953 when all the airliners on the North Atlantic were still piston engine-powered, flogging along through the weather thousands of feet below the 43,000/48,000ft normal cruise of the Canberra.

Above:
This B(I) Mk 8 was supplied to Venezuela in 1957 and returned for overhauls and conversions in 1963 and 1968. It was finally redelivered to Mk 88 standard in 1970; it is seen here at Warton. *British Aerospace*

Below:
A B Mk 2 for Venezuela at Warton in 1965.
British Aerospace

But the advent of the Comet and the 707 on the world air routes was not far away, and air traffic control used the high-flying Canberras as 'ghosts' for the jet airliners which were to come. The US military were also still preoccupied with the problems posed them by the jet bomber, and a National Guard base at Bangor, Maine, sent up Sabres on a practice interception. The crew of the Canberra watched the fighters climbing towards them, and then running out of steam a good 10,000ft below.

Asked to confirm speed and altitude, Hackett replied: 'We're at Mach .78 and 50,000ft, and we've still got some to spare!'

Navigation compared with the inertial systems of today was rudimentary, and there was very little margin for error on the long leg between Preston and Gander, with Goose Bay as the only alternative in range if Gander was out. The two radios each had 10 channels, compared with 600/700 today, and the sets had to be recrystallised on the ground by the crew. The radios, and the ADF sense aerial

were carried outside the pressure cabin so that they were subjected to cold soak of up to −60° for several hours at the heights at which the Canberras flew. This resulted in the 300-mile radio range at the top of the climb rapidly reducing to only 50 miles once the cold took hold.

The main navigation aids on the way were the two Atlantic weather ships Juliet, off the coast of Ireland, and Charlie off Newfoundland. Down the coast of the US there were plenty of beacons, and at Baltimore Friendship, representatives of the Glen L. Martin company who were building the B-57, would come over to help service and despatch the

aircraft. At Jamaica the heat could pose problems during the transit stop, and the ground help could be erratic. Hackett used to make sure that the starter cartridges were kept in the refrigerator of the hotel bar overnight to keep their power.

A request at Warton for 'a few boiled sweets' to suck along the route used to produce 'enough to stock a sweet shop', far more than the crew could cope with, but they then came in handy as 'bribes' down the route for many young 'observers'. But Hackett's main memory was that the Canberra made friends wherever it went, and that he and the other crews always received the greatest help from everybody. After their overnight stops, essential after sectors flown in uncomfortable pressure jerkins (the oxygen supply would be interrupted if the navigator leaned too heavily against his chart table), and with no automatic pilot, there were usually requests for a 'beat-up' of the airfield, which Hackett was usually only too happy to do. Many friends were made in South America as a result of the delivery flights, and particularly in Venezuela where he lived for a year instructing on Canberras. There was at least one aircraft which he not only delivered to the Venezuelans, but which he brought back *twice* over the years to Samlesbury for refurbishing.

Venezuela became the first buyer to come back for more Canberras when, in early 1957, it ordered eight B(I)8s and two T4s. All the B(I)8s were delivered by January 1958, and the second T4 arrived the following month, Hackett and Moneypenny establishing the 19th and final point-to-point Canberra record — between Washington and Caracas.

This country returned for a third time, becoming the first foreign customer for 'refurbished' Canberras. The order on this occasion was for 14, 12 of which were to be B2s and the other two PR3s. Like many other foreign buyers Venezuela sent its Canberras back to Samlesbury for refurbishing, and in 1978 it began modifying its aircraft at home base with a revised radio and armament fit. BAC technicians went out to Venezuela to supervise the work on the first four aircraft, but the Venezuelans completed the remaining aircraft themselves.

France

France placed the second export contract for the Canberra, ordering six B6s in early 1954. This order was unusual in that the French did not want the aircraft directly for air force service as with most of the other overseas customers, but saw them rather as vehicles which they could use for the testing of engines and missiles. Once again the 'diversion' procedure was employed for speedy completion of the order, the first French machine F763, having started life on the assembly line as the tenth RAF B6, WJ763. The next two were supplied under the same plan, but the final three came off the production line in turn. The entire order was completed by 1955, and although B6s had orginally been planned the final two were delivered to B(I)6 configuration. The French employed their Canberras until 1979 in experimental and development projects after which BAe bought back the unused spares.

India

India began to become seriously interested in Canberras during 1956 and discussions on a major order for the IAF took place when the Indian Secretary for Defence visited the UK in June. Once again, EE started work in anticipation of an order, which was duly placed at the start of 1957. The order was for 80, worth around £20million and by far the biggest straight export contract from any source. The Indian order consisted of 65 B(I)58s, eight PR57s and seven T4s. While the T4s were standard trainers, the two other types were much modified to meet the Indian specification although largely based on the B(I)8 and PR7 respectively. The B(I)58 had, for instance, autopilot and additional navigation equipment, while the PR57 had in addition to these modifications a re-worked electrical system and a radio altimeter. India received her first Canberras as early as April, 1957, facilitated by further diversions off the assembly line.

No 5 Squadron of the IAF was the first to take Canberras on to its inventory. This was in 1958, a year in which 38 B(I)58s, two PR57s and two T4s were delivered to the subcontinent. Two further IAF Canberra squadrons, 16 and 35, followed. Final deliveries of the 80 Canberras ordered were in the autumn of 1959, but a further six were ordered in 1961. This order was filled from the 15 which EE had built for stock when it closed the assembly line. India placed an order for a further three Canberras in late 1962. It was filled by ex-RAF aircraft, a T4 and two PR7s modified into PR572, and was completed by the spring of 1964. During 1970, India bought eight B(I)12 and two T13 Canberras being withdrawn from service by the Royal New Zealand Air Force.

Above left:
Two Indian AF B(I)58s on test from Samlesbury in 1959. The Indian order for 80 aircraft was the largest Canberra export order, and also the largest single manufacturing order in Britain at that time from any foreign source. Aircraft series IF909 and IF910.
British Aerospace

Left:
Indian AF Canberras approaching the Taj Mahal.
Indian Air Force photo

119

Pakistan

Pakistan was supplied by the United States with 25 Martin-built B-57s under MDAP (the Military Defence Assistance Plan), the aircraft being promised by President Eisenhower during a visit to Karachi, with a delivery date of September 1959. The aircraft came from the USAF 345th Tactical Bombardment Group on its disbandment, and to meet the deadline the aircraft were delivered without the RB-1A Georgia Peach bombing system which had also been promised by Eisenhower. Nose sections containing the system were later sent to Karachi to replace the standard nose section of the B-57s, standard noses being returned to the US for recycling.

The B-57s equipped Nos 7 and 8 Bomber Squadrons of the 31st Bomber Wing of the Pakistan Air Force, and the aircraft saw action in two subsequent wars, in September 1965, and in December 1971, against India, in both of which there was the ironic situation of each side using Canberras to bomb each other's airfields and installations. Among the weapons deployed by each side were ex-RAF 4,000lb bombs dating from World War 2 and originally intended for the offensive against Germany.

New Zealand

In early 1958, New Zealand placed an order for 11 Canberras, nine B(I)12s (subsequently increased to 11) and two T13s — modified B(I)8s and T4s respectively. Before this order was filled however the Royal New Zealand Air Force received on loan from the RAF 15 B2s which were flown by No 75 Squadron RNZAF from Tengah, Singapore, alongside No 45 Squadron RAF against the Communist guerrillas in Malaya. The first New Zealand B(I)12 was an RAF B(I)8 with autopilot and alterations to navigation equipment, but the rest of the aircraft in the order were new machines off the production line, the last of which was rolled out in November 1959. One of the T13s was a modified T4, the other a new aircraft from the assembly line. While it was waiting for delivery of its trainers, the RNZAF was loaned two RAF T4s during 1959 for crew training at Wigram. No 14 Squadron based at Ohakea operated the B(I)12s. Two of

Below:
The New Zealand B(I) Mk 12. *British Aerospace*

Bottom:
A B(I) Mk 12 for New Zealand over the Wyre Estuary. *British Aerospace*

Above:
A refurbished B Mk 2 for the West German Government, 1966. *British Aerospace*

the aircraft destined for the RNZAF were the last off of the EE production line before it closed down in late 1959.

The B2s on loan from the RAF were returned to the UK shortly after 75 Squadron RNZAF returned home from Malaya. No 75 then operated both B(I)12s and T13s. New Zealand became the first foreign buyer to withdraw Canberras from service. This event occurred in late 1970, when the eight B(I)12s and two T13s still with the RNZAF were replaced by A-4K Skyhawks (one New Zealand B(I)12 had been bought back by BAC). The RNZAF aircraft did not go to the scrap yard, however. They were sold to the Indian Air Force as yet another example of the amazing longevity of the type.

West Germany

Three B2s, ex-RAF, were acquired in 1966 by the West German Government and were used for trials flying by the experimental unit, Erprobungstelle 61, based at Oberpfaffenhofen, near Munich. The aircraft were all delivered in that year after overhaul by Marshalls, of Cambridge, and pre-delivery checks by BAC, at Warton. They were later transferred to the West German Defence Ministry, with civil markings and with cameras in the bomb bay for photo-survey duties including, it is believed, 'peering' over the border into East Germany. In 1977 they reverted to military markings.

Rhodesia

Rhodesia ordered 15 B2s towards the end of 1957. These aircraft did not come from EE however, but were supplied directly by the RAF from its stocks of this mark of the aircraft which was, by this time, being withdrawn from service. Delivery was complete by the middle of June 1959. In addition Rhodesia ordered three T4s, an order which was filled by modifications to B2s which had been phased out by the RAF. The modifications, done at Samlesbury, included fitting new T4 front fuselages and associated equipment.

When an embargo was later placed by Britain on supplies to Rhodesia the flow of spares for the Rhodesian Canberras was cut off, but the servicing gap is believed to have been filled by Atlas Aircraft, South Africa. Rhodesian AF aircraft were fitted locally with rocket rails, and saw action against guerrillas.

Peru

Peru ordered eight B(I)8s during November 1955, and the first of these was delivered in May the following year in charge of the Silver City crew — Hackett and Moneypenny — who had already ferried Canberras to both Venezuela and Ecuador. The first four aircraft for Peru were diversions from orders for the RAF, made up by replacement Ministry of Supply orders. Six Canberras were flown to Peru during 1956, the remaining two following in 1957. Peru ordered one further B(I)8 in 1959 to replace one of the earlier aircraft lost in an accident. Like a number of overseas orders logged at around this time, the order was filled from a stockpile of 15 major assemblies which had been produced to Mark 8 standard before the EE assembly line shut down.

Peru came back in 1965 for six B2s and two T4s, refurbished by BAC. Later that year the country placed its fifth order for Canberras — for one B(I)8, a rebuilt ex-RAF machine which became designated B(I)68 before it was delivered in July 1971. This was the first Mark 8 to be refurbished and sold abroad. Later Peru came back with an order for one T4, and finally put in its seventh order for 12 B(I)8s which were refurbished by both BAC and Marshalls of Cambridge.

Below:
Peruvian B(I) Mk 78 at Warton in November 1960. This aircraft was delivered on 28 November and subsequently crashed on 1 June 1981. *British Aerospace*

Bottom:
A B Mk 2 for Peru with underwing pylons, seen at Samlesbury in 1967. This aircraft was later converted to B Mk 72 standard radio fit. *British Aerospace*

Right:
A Peruvian B Mk 2 over Morecambe Bay. *British Aerospace*

Below right:
20th Anniversary of first flight: some of the original team in front of a B(I) Mk 56 for Peru on 13 May 1969 at Samlesbury. *British Aerospace*

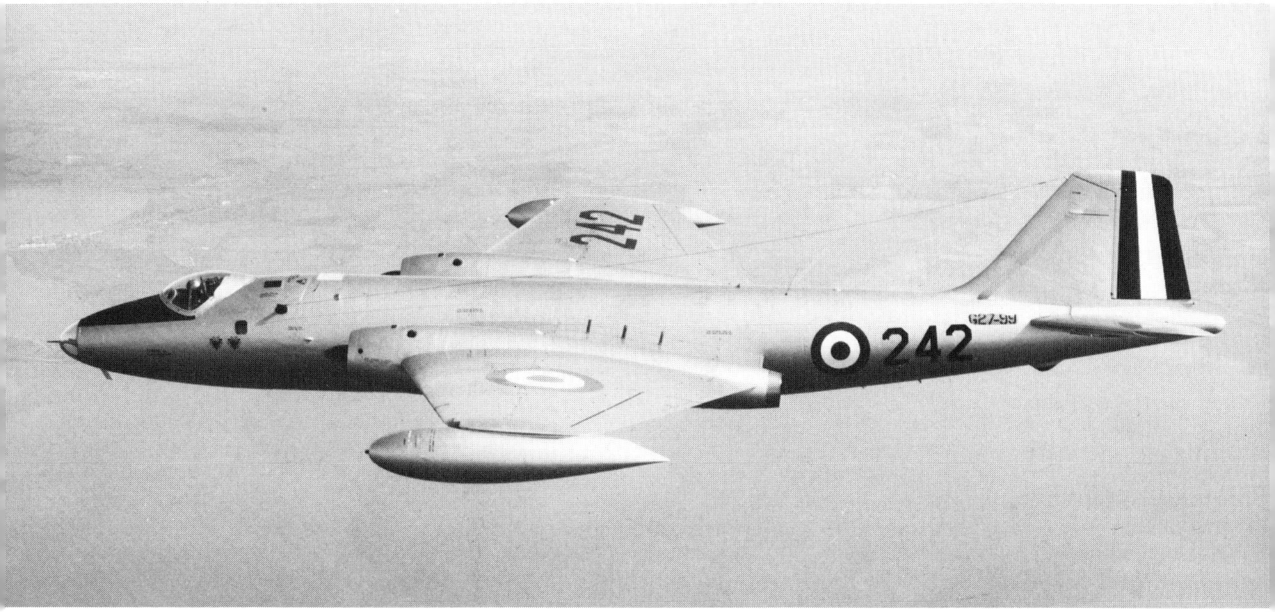
242
G27-99
242

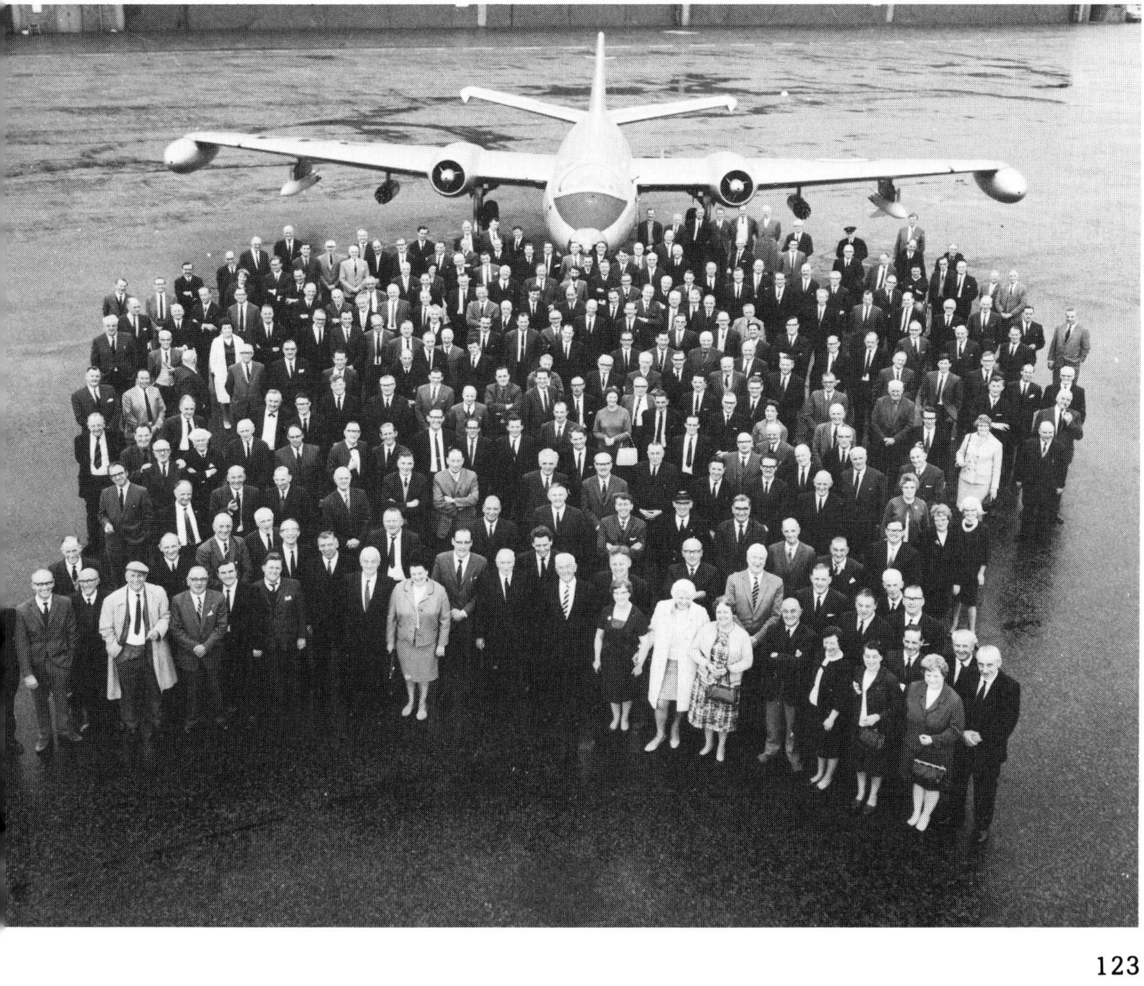

Above:
First aircraft for Argentina on test in primer.
British Aerospace

Argentina

An order for Argentina for refurbished Canberras was announced by BAC concurrently with celebrations to mark the 20th anniversary of the first flight, during which celebrations at Warton Beamont demonstrated the first aircraft destined for the Argentine, a B62 with the Argentine registration B101 and the temporary registration G27-111. The Argentinian order was for 10 B62s and two T64s, and the second B62 was shown at the Farnborough show in the autumn of 1969 with the British civil registration G-AYHP. B101, at Farnborough as a back-up aircraft, was also temporarily on the British civil register with the mark G-AYHO.

Argentinian Air Force crews flew the first three aircraft to their home base from Warton in November 1969, and deliveries were completed by the autumn of the following year. One B62, No B103, was written off in an accident on 22 November 1971.

In the spring of 1982, the Canberras of the Argentinian AF were deployed in a limited way against the country of their manufacture after the Argentine invaded the Falklands in the south Atlantic, and Britain moved to regain the islands. Soon after the invasion the supply of Canberra spares to Argentina was cut off by British Aerospace, and two aircraft at Samlesbury 'frozen' (although refurbishing work went on) on the instructions of the Department of Trade in London. There was, however, no formal restriction on BAe's contract to support Canberras delivered to Peru, and it is likely that Argentina could have obtained spares from that country had she needed them during the Falklands conflict.

The conflict escalated when on 28 April the British Government gave Argentina 48 hours' notice that an air blockade over a 200-mile radius around the Falklands would be imposed to complement the sea blockade, which was already in force. At 4.40am on 1 May the airfield at Port Stanley was bombed by a Vulcan operating with flight refuelling by Victor tankers out of Ascension Island — the first attack by the RAF on a runway since Canberras bombed Egyptian airfields during the Suez operation in 1956. Argentina's response came late that afternoon when a force of Daggers (Israeli-built Mirages) from the mainland attacked RN ships. Two of the fighters were shot down. That evening a formation of three Argentinian Canberras, flying at 50ft, attempted to bomb the British task force ships, but jettisoned bombs on interception. One Canberra was destroyed, the 'kill' being attributed to a Sea Harrier, armed with Sidewinder missiles, of No 801 RN Squadron operating from HMS *Invincible*, and a second claimed as 'severely damaged', also by a Sidewinder, and unlikely to reach its base.

The first engagement highlighted the vulnerability of the Canberra to air-defence missile attack, particularly when operating in daylight in the medium-altitude bomber role. Significantly there were no further reports of Canberra raids until the closing stages of the Falklands war some five weeks later when Canberras were said to be attempting night attacks at low level. During these attacks,

which were believed to have caused no damage or casualties, a second Canberra was reported to have been shot down but the claim was not confirmed. The Ministry of Defence's final list of kills issued shortly after the end of the conflict credits the task force with the destruction of only one Canberra — the one shot down on 1 May.

Summing up, the Argentine Canberra force was able to achieve little during the Falklands campaign up against the defensive weapons of a later era. The aircraft lacked equipment to counter infra-red seeking or radar-guided missiles. The Argentinians were well aware of the lethality of the Sea Harrier and its Sidewinder AIM-9L missiles, operating at night as well as day, and of the Sea Dart area-defence missiles, and were unwilling to commit their Canberras which, without the high speed of their Mirages and Skyhawks, would inevitably have been exposed to high losses

Above left:
Demonstration on 13 May 1969 at Warton to mark the 20th Anniversary. The first Argentine B-62 cleaned up. *British Aerospace*

Left:
Twenty years after the first flight — the Warton demonstration on 13 May 1969. From left to right: Alan Watson, Jack Barlow, Bill Foxcroft, RPB. *British Aerospace*

Below:
The first Argentine aircraft in final finish for delivery seen in June 1969. B Mk 62s from this batch attacked the Falkland Islands task force in May 1982, losing at least one to a Harrier. *British Aerospace*

Above:
A B Mk 52 for Ethiopia on low level tests over the Pennines. *British Aerospace*

Ethiopia

Ethopia became a customer for refurbished Canberras with an order for four rebuilt B2s to B52 standard. Deliveries began in June 1968 and were completed by the end of that year. Ethiopia's experience with Canberras was an unhappy one and included, according to reports reaching Britain, two wheels-up landings, and a pilot absconding in one aircraft to a neighbouring country.

Sweden

An unusual order, for two RAF-retired B2s, was that received in 1959 from Sweden for use on the flight-testing of radars and avionics in general. Similar in appearance to the T11, with a long nose and a radome, they were designated Tp52 by the Swedes, who flew them for 10 years after delivery in early 1960.

Ecuador

Ecuador became the second customer from South America for the Canberra, ordering six B6s in May 1954. Deliveries started about 12

Below:
T11 for Sweden at Warton before delivery in 1960. It was used for trials and training in the Viggen programme. *British Aerospace*

Bottom:
A B Mk 6 for Ecuador, one of six ordered in 1954. *British Aerospace*

months later, and were made with pairs of aircraft. During a flight back to Preston for refurbishing with an Ecuadorian AF crew, one of these aircraft force-landed in Ireland and completed the journey on board a sea ferry. Canberras provided EAF pilots with fast-jet training for the Jaguars which the country bought from Britain in the 1970s.

South Africa
South Africa ordered six Canberras in 1961. These were for B(I)12s, and the order was followed in 1963 by a further order, for three T4s — ex-RAF aircraft. Deliveries of the entire order was completed by early 1964. The aircraft were operated by No 12 Squadron of the SAAF.

Top:
A B(I) Mk 12 for South Africa, one of 12 ordered in 1961. *British Aerospace*

Above:
South African B(I) Mk 12 on test from Samlesbury. These were the last new-built Canberras.
British Aerospace

Below:
A South African T Mk 4 at Samlesbury in 1964.
British Aerospace

20 Record-Breakers

The great leap forward in speed and general performance represented by the Canberra was reflected graphically by the fact that between 1951 and 1958 it set no fewer than 22 world records for distance in time, and height.

The potential of the Canberra in this area was demonstrated on 21 February 1951, when an RAF crew (Sqn Ldr Callard, Flt Lt Haskett and Flt Lt Robson) made, in B2 WD932, what was the first non-stop, non-refuelled crossing of the Atlantic by a jet aircraft, taking 4hr 37min from Aldergrove, Ulster, to Gander, Newfoundland. At an average speed of a little under 450mph it was the fastest-ever Atlantic crossing, but because FAI observers were not there to time the flight it was not possible to claim an official record. This was the aircraft which was demonstrated to the USAF as a result of which the Americans produced the Canberra as the B-57, a story which is recounted in other chapters.

Sadly, also there was no official observance of the delivery flight in August 1951 of the first 'pattern' B2 Canberra on which licence production in Australia was based. That aircraft, A84-307, broke a number of records during the delivery flight from Lyneham, Wiltshire, to Darwin, over 10,240 miles, but once again they could not go into the record books. The Canberra was flown by a Royal Australian Air Force crew of Wing Commander Cumming (pilot) and Flt Lt Harvey (navigator).

Their log reads as follows:
'Wednesday, 1 August 1951, departed UK at 5.20am, arrived Tobruk, Libya, 9.04am in 3hr 44min, distance 1,640nm; departed Tobruk 11.13am, arrived Habbaniya, Baghdad, 1.26pm in 2hr 13min, distance 1,090nm. 2 August, departed Habbaniya, arrived Karachi, in 3hr 22min, distance 1,422nm; departed Karachi, arrived Ceylon in 3hr 16min, distance 1,300nm. 3 August, departed Ceylon, arrived Singapore in 4hr 21min, distance 1,510nm. 4 August, departed

Singapore, arrived Darwin in 4hr 29min, distance 1,810n.

These flights had shown exactly what the Canberra was capable of and when the time arrived for the delivery of the first 'pattern' aircraft to the Martin Corporation in the US, English Electric had FAI observers standing by. The company's confidence was fully justified. Beamont with D. A. Watson as navigator and R. H. T. Rylands as radio operator, flew B2 WD940 from Aldergrove to Gander at an average speed of 481.12mph for the 2,072 statute miles, clipping over two hours off of the previous official fastest East-West crossing of the Atlantic.

On 18 February 1952, a B2 aircraft WD962 established a new official record between London and Castel Benito, Tripoli, Libya, where it subsequently carried out a series of ejector seat trials. It covered the 1,459.83 statute miles in 2hr 41min 49.5sec at an average speed of 538.12mph. The crew was Sqn Ldr L. C. E. Devigne and Flt Lt P. A. Hunt.

Then on 26 August that same year came the best-known of all the Canberra record-making activities — the first double crossing of the Atlantic in one day. This was in the prototype B5 VX185 which, six weeks earlier, had made the first Canberra flight fitted with new rating RA7 Avon engines producing 7,500lb of thrust, 1,000lb more than RA3s which they replaced. Further significant modifications to VX185 were triple-breech cartridge starters instead of the single-breech installation, and integral wing leading-edge fuel tanks. For the record-breaking flight an auxiliary tank was fitted in the bomb bay. A detailed description of the flight is given in Chapter 14. For the record the distance from Aldergrove to Gander and back, 4,144 statute miles, was covered in 10hr 3min 29.28sec for an average speed of 411.99mph, including turn-round time. The West-East Atlantic crossing record established at the same time was 2,072 statute miles covered in 3hr 25min 18.13sec for an average speed of 605.52mph.

Above:
The Canberra is flagged off by the Royal Aero Club at Aldergrove.
British Aerospace

Left:
940 heads into the rain over Loch Neagh towards America.
British Aerospace

Below left:
Landing at Gander 4hr 18min later. *Martin Co*

Bottom left:
The Canberra's crew with the Gander airport manager.
Martin Co

Above right:
940 over the Martin Co Flight Test Centre. *Martin Co*

Right:
R. P. Beamont meets Glenn L. Martin at Baltimore after the Canberra's Atlantic record flight; R. H. T. Rylands is at right. *Martin Co*

Below:
Warton ground staff in support of WD940's Atlantic record on 31 August 1951. Left to right: Jessop, Taylor, Powell, unknown, unknown, Simmons, Barlow, unknown, Whiting, Willacy, Eaves, Potter, Pickthall, Hart, Crombleholme, Atkinson, Manders, Watson, Sharples, Hodson, Ashton, unknown, unknown. *British Aerospace*

Crew: Beamont (captain), Peter Hillwood (second pilot, flying the return leg), Dennis Watson (navigator).

One month later on 28 September 1952, an RAF B2 Canberra established a point-to-point record between London airport and Eastleigh airport, Nairobi, East Africa, covering the 4,239 statute miles in 9hr 55min 16.7sec for an average speed of 427.3mph. Crew; Wg Cdr H. P. Connolly, Sqn Ldr D. Clare, and Air Chief Marshal Sir H. P. Lloyd.

Two further records were obtained in January 1953 by the PR3 prototype VX181 while ferrying to Australia to take part in experimental flying over the Woomera weapons range. The aim was to fly between London and Darwin in less than 24hr, and the 8,608 statute miles distance was in fact covered in 22hr 21.8sec to give an average speed of 391.2mph. The route, over 27/28

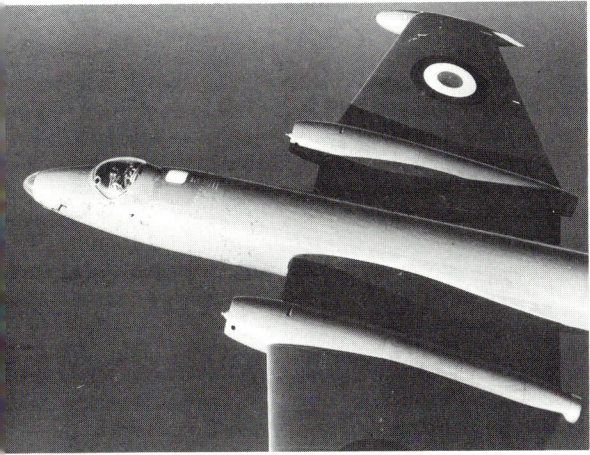

January, was London-Fayid (Egypt) in 4hr 30min (52min on the ground at Fayid), Fayid-Karachi in 3hr 31min (1hr 16min on the ground at Karachi), Karachi-Singapore in 6hr 39min (51min on the ground, Singapore), Singapore-Darwin in 4hr 29min. The second record established on this flight was for the sector between London and Mauripur airport, Karachi, a distance of 3,921 statute miles covered in 8hr 52min 28.2sec for an average speed of 441.8mph. Crew, Flt Lt L. M. Whittington (pilot) and Flt Lt J. A. Brown (navigator).

The year 1953 was the classic for Canberra records, the type setting no fewer than eight including its first official height record. This came on 4 May when, during trials of B2 WD952 which was the flying test-bed for the Bristol Olympus engine, a new world altitude record of 63,668ft was established by W. F. Gibb, the Bristol Aeroplane Company pilot (no observer was carried, to save weight) from the company's airfield at Filton, Bristol. The record was 7.1% better than the previous one which had been set by a Ghost-engined Vampire, built by English Electric and flown by John Cunningham. Thrust rating of the Olympus BO1.99 engines was limited to 8,000lb due to space limitations, from a normal 9,750lb. The altitude record had been exceeded unofficially several times by the same aircraft before the record-breaking sortie.

Three further records went to Canberras during the England-New Zealand air race during early October 1953, which turned into a Canberra benefit after all of the other types originally entered in the speed section were withdrawn for various reasons. The race was won by a PR3, WE139, which like the other British entries was operated by a special flight of No 540 Squadron RAF. In winning the aircraft set two new records, between London and Basra, Iraq, distance 2,832 statute miles, in 5hr 11min 5.6sec for an average speed of 544.3mph; and London-Christchurch, distance 11,796 statute miles in 23hr 50min

Above left:
PR3 prototype XV181 on charge to Boscombe and flown by 'Dick' Whittington for Charles Brown's camera, prior to the London-Australia record in 1953.
Charles Brown via RAF Museum

Left:
Flt Lt Whittington and Flt Lt Brown with PR3 VX181 before their record London-Darwin flight on 27 January 1957. *Charles Brown via RAF Museum*

42sec for an average speed of 494.48mph. The crew was Flt Lt R. L. E. Burton (pilot) and Flt Lt D. H. Gannon (navigator).

The third record during the race went to WH773, the first PR7, which covered the 5,416 statute miles between London and Colombo, Ceylon, in 10hr 25min 21.5sec for an average speed of 519.5mph. The crew was Wg Cdr L. M. Hodges, and Sqn Ldr R. Currie.

The final two Canberra records during 1953 marked the beginning of a remarkable series of flights by WH699, a standard B2 named *Aries 1V* and operated by the RAF Flying College at Manby, Lincolnshire, between that year and 1959. *Aries 1V* established a new London-Capetown record on 17 December, covering the 6,009.72 statute miles in 12hr 21min 3.8sec for an average speed of 486.6mph, and on the return leg on 19 December, set a new Capetown-London record of 13hr 16min 25.2sec for an average speed of 452.8mph. The crew on the London-Capetown leg were Wg Cdr G. G. Petty in command and navigators Sqn Ldrs T. P. McGarry and J. McDonald-Craig, and on the return leg Wg Cdr A. H. Humphrey (later ACM Sir Andrew Humphrey) in command and navigators Sqn Ldrs D. Bower and R. F. B. Powell.

By the end of 1953 the Canberra had became known all over the world as a result of its record-breaking activities.

There was a pause in the setting of new time and distance records during 1954, although on 14/15 October that year *Aries 1V*

became the first British jet aircraft to fly over the North Pole. The flight took 6hr 43min from Bardufoss over the North Pole and back to Bodo, Norway, and the crew was Wg Cdr Humphrey in command and navigators Sqn Ldrs Bower and F. R. Wood. Navigation equipment carried by the Canberra included a GEC radio compass which failed due to icing, Eureka/Rebecca which failed through over-heating, two VHF radio sets, only one of which could transmit and then on only one frequency, a periscope sextant, a hand-held sextant, an air position indicator/air mileage unit and a G4B gyro-magnetic compass.

This was the most headline-catching of a number of Polar navigation flights which *Aries 1V* made during 1954 and 1955. Overnight on 27/28 June in the latter year the aircraft was back among the records again when it streaked from Ottawa to London, a distance of 3,330.416 statute miles in 6hr 42min 12sec for an average speed of 496.825mph. On this occasion Sqn Ldr I. G. Broom was at the controls and the navigators were Sqn Ldrs Bower and R. A. Seymour.

The Canberra hit the world headlines again in August 1955 when a new PR7, WT528, broke three records during the course of a double Atlantic crossing in one day, and W. F. Gibb broke his own altitude record in the Olympus test-bed aircraft out of Filton.

The Atlantic aircraft was flown by J. W. Hackett with P. J. Moneypenny as navigator — a Silver City Airways crew who had been employed by English Electric to make numerous Canberra delivery flights, in particular to South America. This team took WT528 from London to New York, a distance of 3,475.96 statute miles, on 23 August in 7hr 29min 56.7sec at an average speed of

Above:
Wg Cdr G. G. Petty arrives at Capetown after breaking the record from London on 17 December 1953.
British Aerospace via D. Woods

Left:
Capetown-London record, December 1953. The crew of *Aries IV* **from left to right: Sqn Ldr R. F. S. Powell (Nav), Wg Cdr Andrew Humphrey (pilot), Sqn Ldr D. Bower (Nav).**
Air Historical Branch 7242

Below left:
The start of the trans-Polar flight by *Aries IV* **on 20 October 1954; Andrew Humphrey (later Marshal of the RAF, Sir Andrew) with navigators (right) and Norwegian officers (left) at Bardufoss.**
Air Historical Branch 8913

461.12mph, and made the return journey after a refuelling stop of only 35min at New York in 6hr 16min 59.5sec at an average speed of 550.35mph.

The third record was for the round-trip, a distance of 6,915.92 statute miles having been covered in 14hr 21min 45.5sec to give an average speed of 481.52mph.

The record flight naturally remained vividly in the mind of Johnny Hackett, who recalled that the PR7 which was fitted with tankage for the New Zealand air race, including 425gal in tip tanks which were blown off with explosive bolts when empty, left Heathrow but had to 'start' from Croydon to satisfy the city centre-city centre record rules. This entailed overflying Croydon at low altitude — in spite of thick fog so that the observers could start their stop watches, and then out across the Atlantic with navigator Moneypenny singing gently to himself over the intercom, for an eventual straight radar let-down into New York.

The Canberra's arrival created enormous interest and although canvas screens had been erected on the airfield for the crew to retire behind during their quick turnround (the 'loo' in the Canberra was a sort of hot-water bottle, exceptionally difficult to use with bulky flying clothing) Hackett and Moneypenny soon found that American newspaper cameramen were no respecters of such privacy.

Interest back at Heathrow where the Canberra landed after overflying Croydon once more, was even greater with 10,000 people turning out to welcome it Hackett recalled: 'They were great days. The Canberra was a tremendous breakthrough in speed, so much so you could hardly fail to break records with it. We used to joke that going to Blackpool from London in the train — 8½hr in those days — was nearly as long as the flight time between Lancashire and South America by Canberra — 4½hr to Gander, 2hr to Baltimore, 2½hr to Jamaica, and 1½hr to Venezuela.'

Six days later, Gibb took WD952 up to 65,890ft to break his previous record established with the same aircraft two years previously, by over 2,000ft.

Walter Gibb recalled the details of his two record-breaking outings in the article which he wrote for *The Rolls-Royce Magazine*, published in 1982. After the decision had been taken initially to attempt the record the aircraft was modified, mainly through a massive reduction in weight as it was

Above:
Peter Moneypenny and John Hackett before the London-New York-London flight in August 1955. The aircraft is PR7 WY528. *British Aerospace*

calculated that it would climb a further 9in for every pound saved. The observer, his instrumentation, and the camera recorder in the bomb bay, were all removed. 'I even wore sailing shoes instead of flying boots, and the pilot's dinghy was discarded in favour of a balsa wood cushion!' The bomb doors and their operating mechanism were removed and replaced by a lightweight fairing.

After reaching the summit at more than 63,600ft during the first record on 4 May 1953, he started to close the throttles gently but there was a surge and a loud bang from the port engine. It went out followed a second later by the starboard engine . Gibb wrote: 'I then had to blow up my (pressure) suit rapidly,. switch off all the electrics to conserve the battery, and descend as quickly as the aeroplane would allow, because the engines were not generating electrical power, or pressurising the cabin. However, with no power at all, the aeroplane soon got down to 50,000ft. All the handling problems then disappeared, and I had a very gentle and quiet descent to 40,000ft, where the engines were relit.'

For the second sortie, on 29 August 1955, the electrical starters weighing nearly 200lb were removed after the engines had been started for the flight. With both engines on 'maximum continuous' and jet pipe temperatures absolutely on the limit the aeroplane would climb no further, and the altimeter was a few hundred feet short of the record. 'So I eased the throttles forward a bit and exceeded the jet pipe temperature limits

by 50 degrees. The aeroplane climbed the few hundred feet, and I was certain I had beaten the record. I closed the throttles, and descended.'

Back on the ground all the figures were analysed and it was found that he had beaten his own record, 'but only by over-temperaturing the engines, six of the blades on one having been burnt in half . . . a nice touch, the engineering department at Bristol mounted one of the burned blades and presented it to me. I still treasure it.'

One Canberra record was set up in 1956 — from London-Cairo, on 16 February. The aircraft, a B(I)8, was on its way to Aden for tropical trials. The distance of 2,182.6 statute miles was covered in 3hr 57min 18.9sec for an average speed of 551.8mph. The crew on this occasion was Peter Hillwood and D. A. Watson.

Above:
B Mk 2 WD952 was modified by Bristol's as a flying test bed for the Olympus engine. *British Aerospace*

Below:
Walter Gibb flying the altitude record aircraft.
British Aerospace

Hackett and Moneypenny established three unofficial point-to-point records in May that year while ferrying the first Canberra for Peru — No 747, previously WT343 — by way of Gander, Baltimore, Jamaica and Panama.

Manby came back into the news on 25 May 1957, when Canberra *Aries V*, WT528, a PR7, established a new record between Tokyo and London. The aircraft took off from Haneda airport and routed by way of Alaska, northern Canada, and across the North Atlantic before landing at West Malling aerodrome,

Kent, a distance of 5,942.5 statute miles. The journey was completed in 17hr 42min 2.4sec for an average speed of 335.7mph. The aircraft commander was Wg Cdr W. Hoy, and the crew, Flt Lts P. J. Lageson and J. S. L. Denis.

Then on 28 August that year Gibb's altitude record in the Bristol Olympus Canberra was surpassed by a Canberra being operated by Napiers to flight-test the company's Double Scorpion rocket engine. The aircraft, WK183, was flown by M. Randrup, chief test pilot of Napier, from Luton and the rocket engine was brought in at 44,000ft on the climb. With this additional boost the Canberra climbed to a record 70,310ft, beating the previous record height by well over 4,000ft. With the pilot on this occasion was test observer Walter

Shirley, the flight development engineer in charge of Scorpion trials (see Chapter 21).

Aries V, the RAF Flying College aircraft mentioned above, set the last great Canberra record when, on 22 February 1958, it covered the 2,062.39 statute miles between Friendship airport, Washington DC and Maiquetia airport, Caracas, Venezuela, in 4hr 10min 59.7sec for an average speed of 491.9mph. *Aries V* was, in fact, the PR7 WT528 which three years earlier on English Electric charge, had made the double Atlantic crossing to New York and back in one day. It was delivered to Manby in June 1956, and flew to many parts of the world on long-range RAF navigational training flights. The aircraft commander on the delivery flight to Caracas and the VAF was John Hackett.

Above:
Hillwood and Watson with the ground crew and their B(I) Mk 8 for the London-Cairo record in 1956. Left to right: Thompson, Lund, Hillwood, Southern, Watson, Taylor, Gregson, Barlow, Smith; front Lawrenson, Fitton, Powell, Hawthornthwaite.
British Aerospace

Right:
PR7 WT528 as *Aries V* set a new record from Tokyo-London, 25 May 1957. *British Aerospace*

Top:
Preparing to fly the altitude record breaker. The Scorpion rocket equipped WK183. Randrup and Shirley are in partial pressure equipment with RAE/GQ fixed-visor helmets. *Napier*

Above left:
WK183 firing its Scorpion rocket motor. This aircraft set a new world record at 70,310ft on 28 August 1957 flown by Randrup and Shirley. *Napier*

Above:
The only way into the fixed visor helmet to release differential pressure in the ears was by use of sugartongs! *Napier*

Left:
The Napier flight team at Cranfield; left to right: Ken Cartwright, Mike Randrup, Walter Shirley, Tommy Lampitt. *Napier*

137

21 Special Duties

So docile, steady, free of vices, and easy to keep serviceable was the Canberra that it soon became clear that it would provide an excellent platform for all manner of special duties. For the aircraft and engine manufacturing companies the aircraft was the answer to a long-felt want, for they were developing a new generation of powerplants and missiles and lacked a test vehicle for them capable of prolonged high-speed flight at altitudes of 40,000ft or more.

The Canberra fitted that bill, and although the squadrons of RAF Bomber Command were anxious to get their hands on their new charge, more than half of the B2s which came off the assembly line in the first full year of production, 1951, were allocated to Government and industrial research establishments. WD947 was used by RAE Farnborough for meteorological flights, and WD931, WD954 and WD962 went to the same establishment. WD930 and WD943 were used to test Avon jet engines, WD933 to test Sapphires, and WD952 to test the Olympus. WD937, WD956, WD958 and WD959 were all kept by English Electric for development duties. It was the beginning of a trend, with Canberras due to figure for more than 30 years in a wide spectrum of research and development programmes. At the 1952 Farnborough air show three engine manufacturers had Canberras on display, in addition to two under the English Electric banner!

The third prototype B1, VN828 was fitted during 1954 with a longer nose and a large radome by Boulton Paul Aircraft for use by the Telecommunications Research Establishment at Defford for research flights which began from the middle of the following year.

In the early 1950s official interest in the potential of small rocket motors for boosting military aircraft to altitudes above the limitations of their air-breathing jet engines was manifested in the developments of the Scorpion liquid rocket motor at Napiers and the Spectre at de Havilland; and in 1956 Canberra B2 WK163 and the second B1 prototype VN813 were allocated to the programme as flying test beds, with the Scorpion being specified as additional power for the new English Electric Lightning supersonic fighter.

Below:
A reheat system for the Avon engine was tested in B Mk 2 WD943 at Rolls-Royce, Hucknall, in the early 1950s. The reheat 'petals' can be seen on the port tailpipe.
Rolls-Royce

At Luton flight development engineer Walter Shirley was in charge of Scorpion testing and visitors were impressed by his apparently considerable confidence in the system when they were required to watch him operate test-firings from a control stand alongside the rocket with virtually no practical protection. The visitors could view these proceedings from behind the blast wall with an armour-glass window — if, as Shirley put it, they so wished!

The Scorpion proved technically reliable in ground testing, and in its initial flight trials in WK163 in May that year carried out by Mike Randrup and Shirley, it was equally successful.

Randrup, for many years the quietly-precise chief test pilot of Napiers, assisted by Ken Cartright and Tommy Lampitt with Walter Shirley as flight engineer, flew the

Above:
B Mk 2 WD822 on test from Bitteswell as a test-bed for the Armstrong Siddeley Sapphire engine in 1953.
British Aerospace

trials on WK163 with the rocket motor, and in its finally developed 'Double Scorpion' form on WK163 Randrup and Shirley took it to a new official world record of 70,310ft on 28 August 1957; at this point the margin of controllability of the Canberra between stalling and the compressibility boundary was less than 10kts — an operation demanding a high degree of skill and knowledge of the aircraft by Randrup and confident support by his flight engineer.

Soon however the remarkable capabilities of the English Electric Lightning fighter were being demonstrated to show that well over 65,000ft could be achieved operationally on

Left:
Final task for the prototype B Mk 2. VX165's rear fuselage with the Napier 'Double Scorpion' installation being test-fired at Luton in 1957. *Napier*

Avon RA24 power alone in energy-climb semi-ballistic trajectory from a Mach 2 run at the tropopause, Jimmy Dell reached 75,000ft on test from Warton in Lightning Mk 3 XN734 on 7 March 1964; and when successful intercepts were carried out by RAF Lightnings of U-2 aircraft of the USAF at extreme altitudes over UK (much to their surprise!) the Scorpion rocket installation was seen to be no longer necessary and the project was cancelled.

Double Scorpion installations were however made in two B6 Canberras on No 72 Squadron Hemswell for special purposes and one of these was used successfully for sampling the atomic cloud of the Christmas Island nuclear tests in 1957.

Shortly after this in April 1958 one of these aircraft suffered a rocket motor incident at extreme altitude over UK and the crew, Flt Lts de Salis and Lowe, made successful Martin Baker ejections at approximately 56,000ft and survived the long free fall to 10,000ft where their parachutes opened automatically with only minor injuries and some frost bite.

This was believed to be the highest-ever escape at that time, and it said much for the effectiveness of their pressure helmets and partial pressure suit survival equipment developed by the enthusiastic specialists of the RAF Institute of Aviation Medicine at Farnborough in the early 1950s.

The de Havilland Spectre programme was also technically successful as the first fully throttlable rocket engine, and after reallocation of VN813 from TRE to de Havillands in 1953 as a flying test bed flying began on 18 December 1956. But then a hitch

Right:
The second B Mk 1 prototype powered by R-R Nene engines in enlarged nacelles. It is seen here on DH Spectre rocket trials at Hatfield. *British Aerospace*

Below:
The second B Mk 1 prototype on test from Hatfield with the DH Spectre rocket motor.
British Aerospace

Above:
U10 unmanned target 'drone' on a piloted test flight from the maker's airfield — Short Bros, Sydenham, Belfast.
British Aerospace

occurred. De Havilland naturally saw their rocket motor as competitive with the Scorpion, but when they began to explore the high altitude performance of their engine they found that progress was limited by the airframe Mach limit of VN813. Even though since its earliest flying, the bulbous Nene engine installations had resulted in Mach limitation of 0.05 lower than the B Mk 2s; this had apparently escaped those responsible for R&D allocations, and in due course a formal request was received at Warton for a report and recommendations on the 'rogue' characteristics of VN813. Unfortunately the only recommendation which could be made was that VN813 should be replaced by a standard B2, but the timescale did not justify this and so the Spectre was not able to attempt an altitude record although its general technical development was completed satisfactorily.

The Canberra's excellent high-altitude performance made it ideal for rocket-motor trials, and it was for this same reason that it was pressed into service during that same year, 1956, in support of British atomic bomb tests at Maralinga, Australia. A special flight of six B6s was formed to make a series of flights near the mushroom clouds formed after the explosions, collecting dust samples through air filters built into modified wing tanks. Two of the six aircraft, which were operated by No 76 Squadron RAF, were fitted with the Double Scorpion rocket engine to enable them to collect samples at even higher altitude than the others. Four PR7s flown by No 100 Squadron RAF were later used to make sampling flights after hydrogen bomb tests at Christmas Island, in the South Pacific.

The first U10 version of the Canberra — an unpiloted target drone — appeared from the Belfast works of Short Brothers and Harland in May 1957. This was WJ624, a modified B2 withdrawn from RAF service, and the plan was to use it in development trials of guided weapons. First trials with WJ624 had a pilot in the aircraft and flying it through a supervisory panel installed in the cockpit. This panel simulated, through push buttons, the 13 inputs which were eventually to be sent to the aircraft in pilotless mode over a radio link.

In a second stage the radio link was introduced to control the Canberra, but with a pilot flying in the aircraft in a supervisory capacity and ready to take over in case of any systems failure. This stage was reached in 1958 and a second U10, WJ987, was used at Royal Aircraft Establishment Bedford.

U10s went into service in 1959, the first being WD961. The majority of them were despatched to the Woomera weapons-testing range in Australia, where the first ground-controlled flight of a pilotless Canberra took place on 25 June that year. The aircraft were used as targets in the trials of several new British missiles being developed at that time including one from the same 'stable' as the Canberra, the English Electric Thunderbird.

Most firings were made without warheads, but some were live and resulted in the destruction of aircraft. A total of 17 U10s went to Woomera, and a further six were sent to 728B Squadron of the Fleet Air Arm based

Top:
WH734 operating from the FR Ltd airfield at Tarrant Rushton with a trial installation of a drogue system for RAF tankers.
Flight Refuelling Ltd

Above:
T11 VN828, radar trainer for Javelin conversion training, seen at Warton prior to delivery to 228 OCU in 1959.
British Aerospace

Left:
The Ferranti 'Airpass' intercept radar for the Lightning supersonic fighter was flight-tested from Edinburgh in this modified B Mk 8 in the late-1950s. *Ferranti*

at Malta, for operations connected with the development of Seacat and Seaslug anti-aircraft missiles. These six were fitted with PR9 hydraulic flight controls and were designated U14. The first pilotless flight was by WH720 in August 1961, and in the trials that followed one aircraft, WH921, was shot down by HMS *Girdle Ness*. All of the surviving Canberra drones were eventually returned to the UK for storage. By that time they had been redesignated D10s and D14s.

Canberras were used for many years to test ejector seats in the Martin Baker programme, and in-flight refuelling equipment and techniques by Flight Refuelling Ltd. In 1959/60 a special flight of six was assembled by RAE Farnborough to take part in Operation 'Swifter' which was a series of low-altitude, high-speed flights in Libya to investigate turbulence encountered under those conditions, in support of the TSR2 programme.

Gradual withdrawal from RAF operational roles meant that there were plenty of aircraft available for special duties, a fact of which Government departments and aerospace companies took full advantage. It was estimated that in 1961 no fewer than 20 such organisations were flying up to 50 Canberras on development work. Not all were 'second-hand', however. De Havilland had a new PR9 delivered in late 1961 (coded the SC9 after modification by Short Brothers and Harland) for trials with the Red Top air-to-air missile. Boulton and Paul carried out trial installa-tions of the Nord AS30 air-to-ground missile on WH967 in early 1962.

One of the few Canberras to carry British civil registrations was WD937, the ninth production B2, which was used by English Electric for tasks in support of the Canberra, Lightning and TSR2 programmes. WD937 was used to flight-test various trial installa-tions, including the power-controlled rudder for the PR9, for air-to-air photography, for weather flights, as a chase 'plane, and for selecting suitable low-level routes for TSR2 trials. Its civil registration was G-ATZW, a mark carried from 1966 until 1968, when the aircraft was withdrawn from service.

The Canberra was still being used as a development workhorse as late as 1982 when a specially-converted aircraft was used to fly in front of the second development BAC146 feederjet airliner prototype G-SSHH, producing a water spray comparable to natural icing conditions. The tests demonstrated that the 146 was able to tolerate a significant amount of ice on its aerofoil leading edges, and that its de-icing equipment could remove any build-up quickly.

Below:
The RAE meteorological research flight flew this PR3 for high level research including dust sampling between 1964 to 1981. *MoD*

22 New Canberras for Old

The longevity of the Canberra could best be appreciated in No 2 Shed at British Aerospace, Samlesbury, where aircraft were refurbished and reconditioned for the RAF and foreign air forces in a continuous programme from 1960 through to 1982.

The machines arrived in a wide variety of conditions, some with plenty of life left in them, others — having stood for years in the open in maintenance units — with clearance to make only the one delivery flight to BAe; a few so far deteriorated that they arrived on low-loaders by road or, as was the case with two South American users, in the belly of a Super Guppy transport aircraft.

Samlesbury's refurbishing work over the years fell into two main areas — Canberras being reconditioned 'as new' from disused RAF stocks for purchase by foreign air forces, and similar work on aircraft already on the inventories of the RAF and air forces abroad for 'return to service'. In the former case BAe sent teams to RAF MUs to survey Canberras stored there. Their brief was to assess hours flown and fatigue suffered by individual aircraft and then, like buyers in a used-car showroom, to select the best.

Canberras arriving back at Salmesbury were often in an extremely poor state, paint faded, oil leaking, and corrosion evident. Their first treatment was to be jacked up with wheels and bomb bays lowered, and then drained of all fluids so that an acceptance check could be made. Then the flying controls were stripped out with the serial numbers of every part carefully noted. Every item from a particular aircraft was stored in boxes alongside, the rule being that individual machines received their own parts back wherever possible.

After the aircraft had been stripped, paint remover was sprayed on and left to stand before a high-powered water jet was applied.

Below:
Time-expired aircraft awaiting overhaul at Samlesbury during the Canberra refurbishing programme 1960-1982. *British Aerospace*

This had the effect of paring the Canberra down to its bare metal. It was then towed into the production hangar where the work of disassembly began. The engines were removed and sent away for new-life overhaul, either to an MU if the aircraft belonged to the RAF or to Rolls-Royce at East Kilbride, Scotland where they were made originally in the case of a foreign aircraft.

Then the wings were removed followed by the tailplane and the fin. The fuselage was then split into three and the parts spread between the various shops. Fuel tanks, undercarriage, piping, hydraulics and cockpit instrumentation all came out. Separate parts of the airframe then went to the spray shops for stripping inside, and then into a facility where they were vacuum blasted. This process reached every internal corner, removed any trace of corrosion, and left clean metal which was then given a thin coat of etch primer to prevent deterioration. By this stage each aircraft had been in the works for about five weeks.

Assessors then closely inspected the disassembled aircraft — made up originally of 46,000 different parts, and with 12,000 active spares items in the BAe stores in 1982 — and decided which sections could be saved and which should be discarded. Updating modifications, and special items asked for by foreign customers were identified and planned in at this stage.

The biggest decision which was made at this time on each aircraft was whether a new centre spar was required. This is the heavy forging to which the wings are attached, and although its replacement was described by one Canberra worker as being akin to a heart transplant for the aircraft, Samlesbury perfected a difficult and complicated production-change technique over the years. With a new centre spar Canberras were guaranteed a new life of 10 years with a major overhaul after six years, and some aircraft came back and had the 'operation' at Samlesbury twice within their lifetime.

To fit the new main spar forging a repair scheme was evolved in which the centre section of the fuselage was split in half horizontally. The technique was pioneered by foreman Ian Warnock and fitter Kevin Woods in a period of trial and error, and it was put into operation from 1968. Reconditioning the Canberra wings was also a difficult job as they could not be stripped down out of jig in case they deformed. Instead, they had to be rebuilt in progressive stages.

Taking it all apart, reconditioning, and then putting it all back together again took around 12 months for each aircraft — up to six months longer if it was a foreign airforce aircraft and there were special modifications to be incorporated. At the end of it all, a beautiful 'new' aircraft would emerge from No 2 Shed, paint gleaming inside and out, all electrics replaced and other systems refur-

Below:
Fully dismantled Canberras beginning rebuild at Samlesbury 1970. *British Aerospace*

Above:
An overhauled T Mk 7 is prepared for flight testing.
British Aerospace

Below:
Three refurbished aircraft — for West Germany, Peru and Venezuela — at Warton on 21 September 1966.
British Aerospace

bished so that to the untutored eye they looked as if they were new.

Then followed a comprehensive series of tests including engine runs, synchronisation of systems, quality control, compass swings, and the weighing of the aircraft. After that came the new 'maiden' flight to the original test schedule with a pilot from the BAe company flight operations centre at Warton at the controls; and after the debriefing which followed any snags were distributed to the various shops for rectification. After a series of further test flights, usually three, in 'clean' configuration, the Canberra was trimmed for tip tanks. Radar and weapons systems were checked, and the aircraft was flown again. Only at that stage was the final paint finish applied to the exterior — a process which could take around one week. There was then a despatch inspection when cowls and leading-edge panels were removed to make sure there were no leaks (the fuel tanks were given exhaustive leak tests during the strip-down period), after which the owning or purchasing air force were notified that their aircraft was ready for collection.

The export programme of new, and ultimately rebuilt and overhauled Canberras was still active in 1982 after 30 continuous years, and comparison of the total value of Canberra exports with the procurement costs of 30 years of Canberra operation in the RAF makes interesting reading.

British Aerospace records to June 1982 showed the total costs of Canberra research and development and production for the RAF were £134million, whereas the value of Canberra exports to 15 countries in the first 21 years up to May 1970 had been £135million. So that irrespective of the subsequent runaway inflation of the 1970s, or of the substantial overseas overhaul contracts of the 1970-82 period, the Canberra had already by 1970 more than paid for itself — a significant commentary on the argument relentlessly put forward by some politicians on the alleged 'profligate squandering' of national wealth on defence.

23 Ultimate Canberra

In 1959 following the success of the B Mk 8 series in the RAF and overseas air forces there was considerable interest in further development of the low-level capability, and Warton produced a design study numbered P28 for a variant with significantly improved penetration speed and range at low level and with essential improvements in ride comfort and fatigue life.

Based on the bomber version of the Mk 8 it was to have a longer nose (side-hinged from the PR9) housing radar and a forward-facing navigator's station with ejection seat; the opening pilot's canopy of the PR9; six feet of wingtip removed each side, three axes irreversible power-operated controls and 500gal wingtip fuel tanks.

Provision was made for Rolls-Royce RA24 engines of 11,250lb st, or RA29s of slightly less power but higher fuel economy.

Maximum weight was to be 55,996lb in bomber configuration, of which 28,302lb was basic equipped weight with 23,294lb fuel and 8,000lb of weapons; or increased weapons load with less fuel.

Still with a modest wing loading, altitude performance and manoeuvrability would have remained good and the power controls would have provided crisp and powerful response at the much-increased target penetration speed of 500kts IAS.

A similar weight of sophisticated reconnaissance equipment provided an alternative role, and there is little doubt that this 'Can-

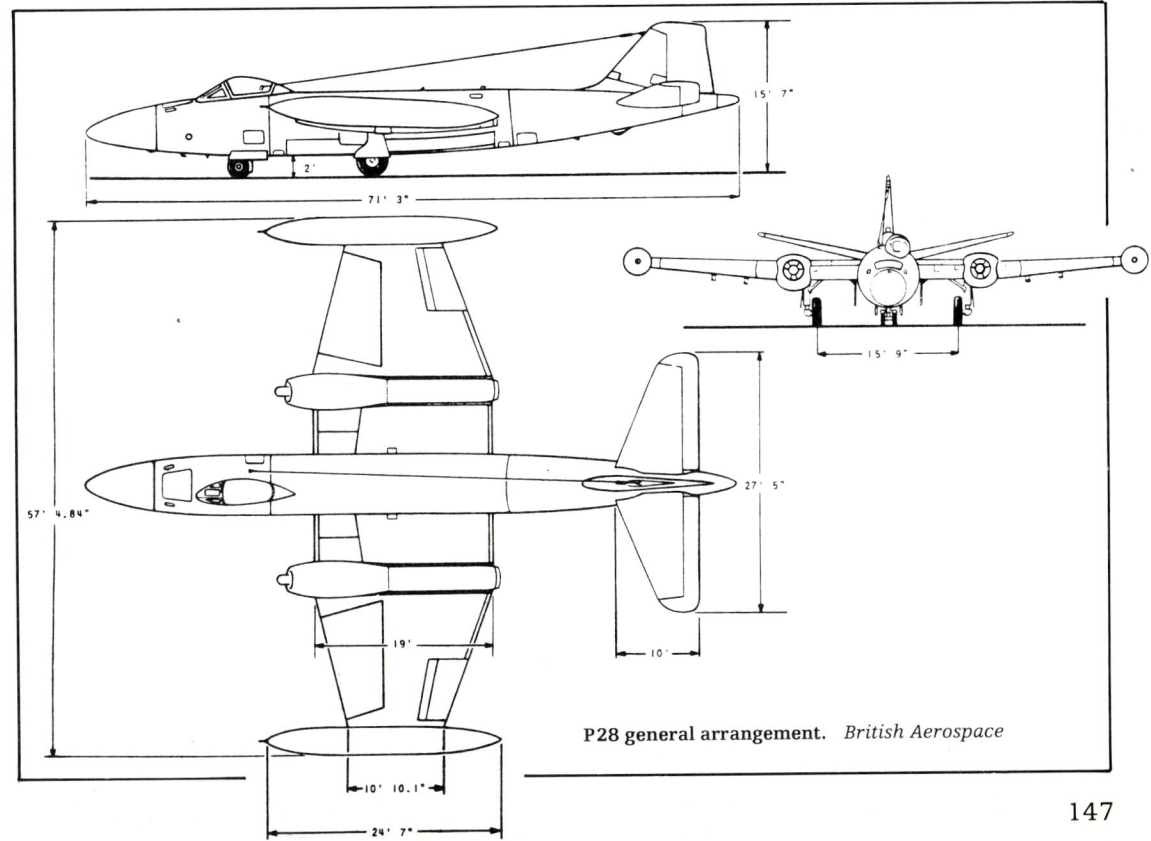

P28 general arrangement. *British Aerospace*

berra' could have provided a valuable Mk 8 replacement role for Nato followed by significant export sales; but in the early 1960s the prevailing climate of opinion in Whitehall was 'swept wings for everything' and the promised higher penetration speeds (though with lower radius of action) of the Buccaneer and the just beginning to emerge designs for the Anglo-French variable geometry aircraft which was eventually cancelled before it got

properly started, were collectively proving more enticing to the inmates of the operational requirements branch of the Air Ministry. Moreover English Electric/BAC were not interested in private venture development so the P28 never emerged, but the Canberra continued successfully for the next $2\frac{1}{2}$ decades although underdeveloped and with potential never fully realised in its country of origin.

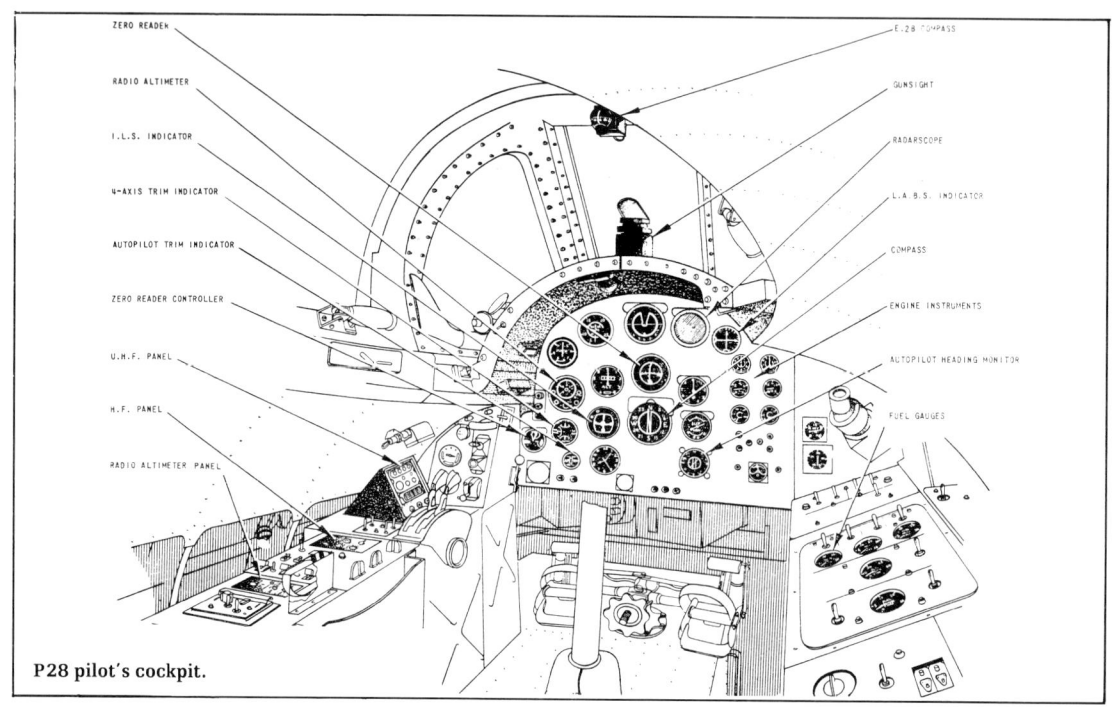

P28 pilot's cockpit.

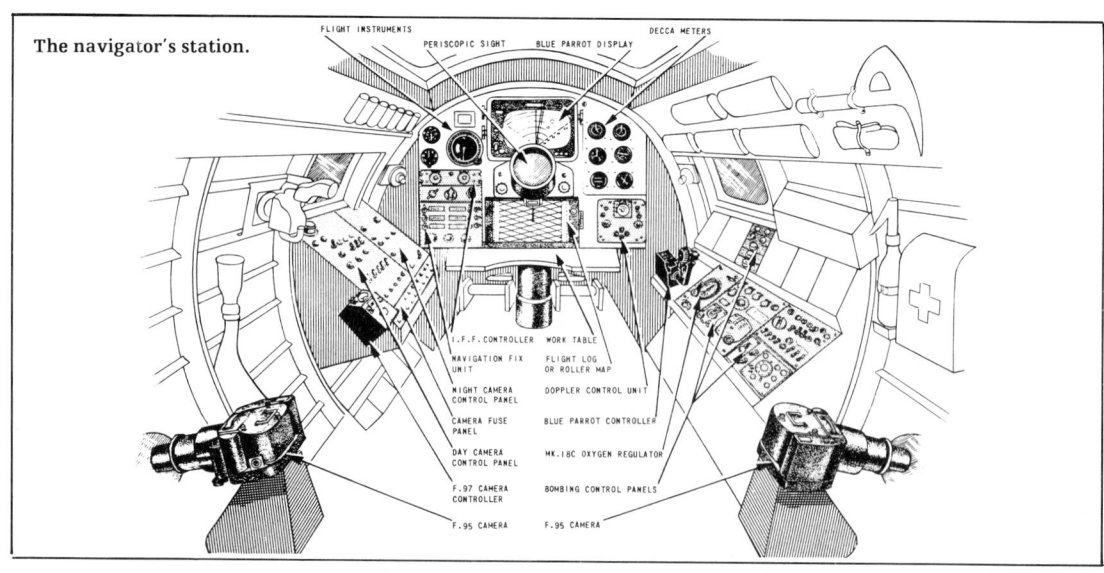

The navigator's station.

24 Conclusion

By any standards one of the world's most successful military aircraft the Canberra is now certain to see 40 years of service and to join the Douglas DC-3 as one of the longest-serving aircraft in aviation history.

How did this happen? What was its secret? These are questions often asked even by members of the profession, for as long ago as its debut in 1949 the basic shape and concept of the Canberra seemed by many too prosaic to raise much interest. But it was in this very 'ordinariness' that the secret lay.

To some of those close to the subject in the early postwar years there was an increasing awareness that the then fashionable trend towards gaining speed by reducing wing span and therefore profile drag, which had evolved during the later developments in propeller-driven aircraft with their heavy 2,000-3,000hp engines at the end of World War 2, was going in the wrong direction. With the significant increases in power-to-weight ratio of the new turbojet engines then becoming available, it seemed to EECo that it might well be practical to exploit the situation by reversing the trend towards ever higher wing loadings with their associated penalties of manoeuvre and altitude limitation; but this thinking was by no means universal, and in the 1945-50 period the first generation jet developments almost invariably suffered the consequences of higher wing loadings than their immediate propeller-driven predecessors.

The specification B3/45 was evolved round the requirement for M0.7 cruise at 42,000ft with specified weapons load and range capability, and this when related to the proposed available engine power defined the wing and power loading quite closely. The only remaining uncertainty was the aerodynamics which would have to be clever to ensure that drag did not defeat the whole exercise.

With a smooth-surfaced high-fineness-ratio structure including symmetrical wing and tail aerofoil sections to optimise the Mach or compressibility performance, profile drag was not seen as the major problem, but induced drag was.

To operate at altitudes substantially above 40,000ft it was seen that a very modest wing

Left:
PR3 VX181 over the Channel at dusk.
Charles Brown (?) via D. Woods

149

loading would be necessary, and it was this coupled with the far-sighted brilliance of Petter's small team at Preston that resulted in the evolution of a classically simple twin-engine layout with smooth aerodynamic lines totally unencumbered with bumps and excrescences, and with a deep, strong wing-box structure held down to a commendably low thickness/chord ratio by its unusually low aspect ratio to give the required low wing loading coupled with low drag.

Added logically to this prescription was a strict policy for conventional manual controls and well-proven systems engineering, all selected to the highest current standards of performance and reliability and none involving exceptionally advanced or unproven experimental equipment. The result was a simple-to-operate-and-maintain bomber aircraft with in general terms the performance and manoeuvrability of a fighter, but with at least a 10,000ft altitude superiority over any other military aircraft of its time.

The Canberra was in fact a classic example of the successful application of the best existing knowledge and experience to a new project in combination with inspired appreciation of the essential design compromise. It was not a radical advance in appearance and for many the absence of swept wings made it look old-fashioned. But there was nothing old-fashioned about its performance or the way in which it accepted hundreds of different roles in the years ahead in the service of many of the world's air forces.

Pilots without exception enjoyed its relaxed and trouble-free operation, and in the 1980s there were many young men flying Canberras whose fathers had flown Canberras before them.

One other aspect of the Canberra story is noteworthy. The development and introduction into Royal Air Force and world-wide service was carried out in an atmosphere of total unified effort at the Preston, Samlesbury and Warton factories, in which there was no element of industrial strife. At all levels of activity, shop floor, design office, administration, development engineering and flight testing, there was an impressive momentum of unquestioning teamwork — if the job needed doing it was done — at any hour of the day or night.

This morale as much as any other single factor accounted for the success of the Canberra and of the commercial success of English Electric Aviation in the 1950s.

The total work force were united with a clear target to build in the Northwest not just the best British but the world's best military aircraft.

It was a good formula and the Canberra was the first measure of their achievement.

Left:
Indian B Mk 58s on test from Samlesbury. *British Aerospace*

Above right:
32 years of Canberra flight testing at Samlesbury: the first Argentine in 1969. *British Aerospace*

Right:
The outcome of the inspiration of W. E. W. Petter and the engineers of the north-west: Preston's air force over the Fylde coast in 1978. From right to left: Canberra, Lightning, Strikemaster, Jaguar, Tornado.
Warton Flight Operations and Photographic Dept

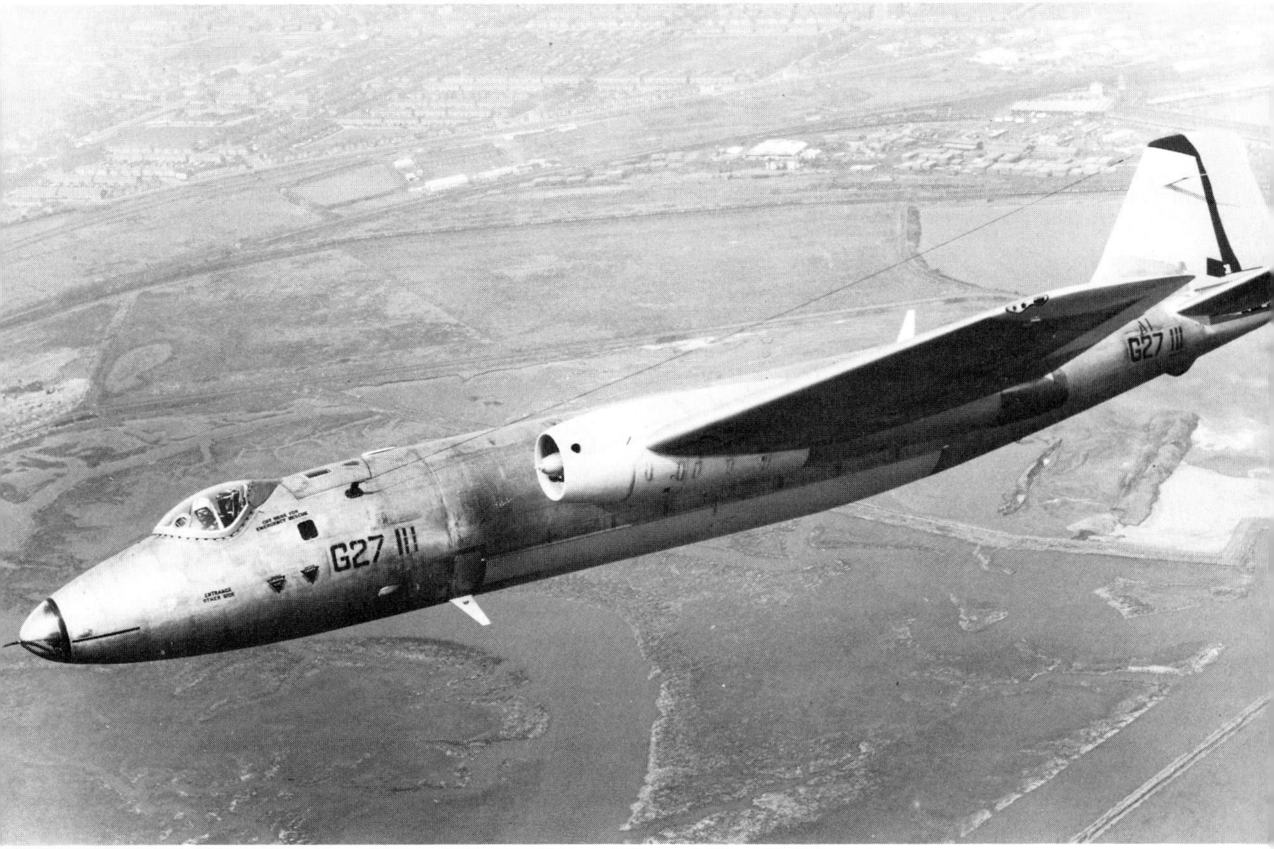

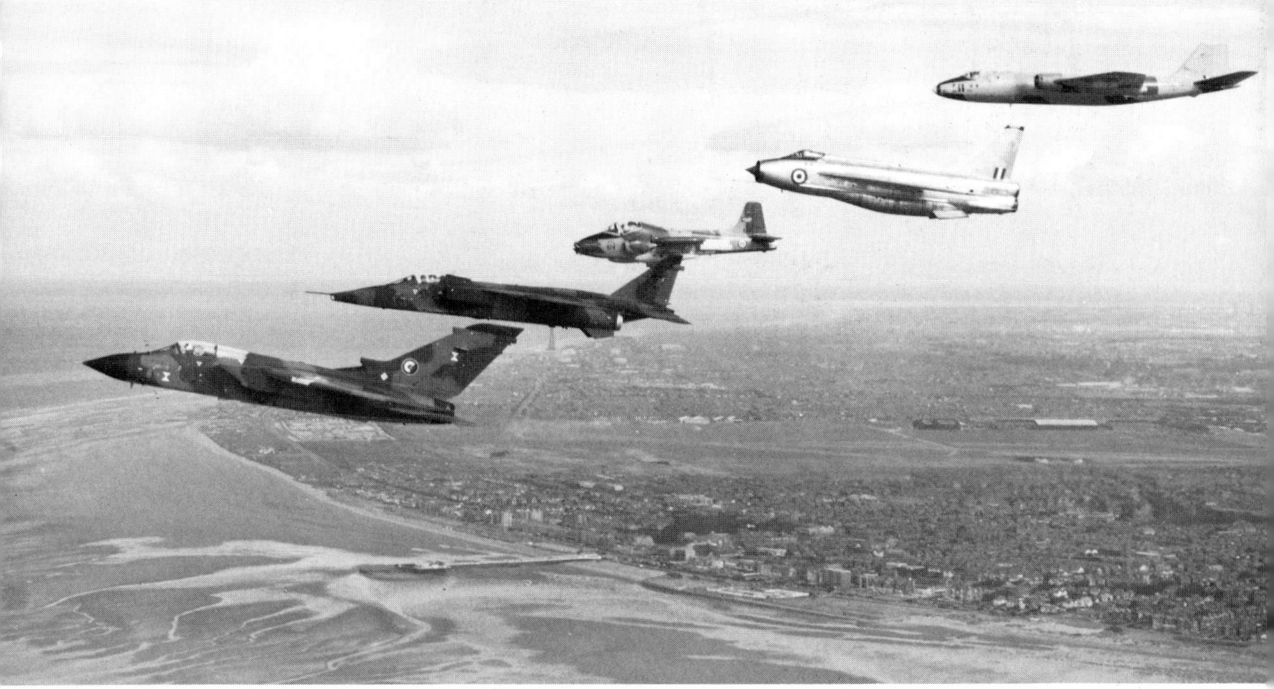

Appendices

1   Main Canberra Marks and Variants

Main Canberra Marks and Variants

B Mk 1	bomber prototype
B Mk 2	high altitude bomber
PR3	photographic reconnaissance
T Mk 4	dual control trainer
B Mk 5	interdictor prototype
B Mk 6	high altitude bomber
B(I) Mk 6	interdictor
PR7	photographic reconnaissance
B(I) Mk 8	interdictor
HA PR9	photographic reconnaissance
U 10	pilotless target aircraft
T 11	radar trainer
D Mk 14	similar to U10; PR9 controls
B Mk 15	development of B6 with integral wing tanks
E Mk 15	avionics update of B Mk 15
B Mk 16	further B6 conversion; use in Middle and Far East
T Mk 17	electronics counter measures
TT Mk 18	target tug
T Mk 19	T11 with modified radar
Mk 22	PR7 with Buccaneer radome

Note: This was the main 'family tree' in the UK, from which various other variants of the Canberra for use both at home and by foreign buyers, and manufacture in the US and Australia, sprang.

Foreign variants supplied from the UK

Argentina B62 and T64
Ecuador B6
Ethiopia B52
France B6
Germany B2
India T4, PR57, B(I) 58, B(I) 66, PR67, B(I) 12*, T13* and TT418
New Zealand B(I) 12 and T13
Peru B(I) 56, B72, T74, B(I) 78 and B(I) 68
Sweden B2
South Africa T4 and B(I) 12
Venezuela B82, B(I) 82, PR83, T84 and B(I) 88
Zimbabwe/Rhodesia B2 and T4

Note: * indicates aircraft originally supplied to New Zealand.

Built abroad under licence

Australia B20 and T21
United States B-57 and variants (also supplied from US to Pakistan and Taiwan)

2   Serial Numbers of UK-built Canberras

RAF Production Summary

The following were built against RAF orders, including some diverted for export without seeing RAF service.

4	VN799, 813, 828, 850	Prototypes
4	VX165, 169, 181, 185	Pre-production
70	WD929-966, 980-999, WE111-122	B2
27	WE135-151, 166-175	PR3
8	WE188-195	T4
18	WF886-892, 907-917	B2
7	WF922-928	PR3
2	WG788-789	B2
86	WH637-674, 695-742	B2

1	WH772	PR3
23	WH773-780, 790-804	PR7
12	WH839-850	T4
60 (S)	WH853-887, 902-925, 944	B2
40 (S)	WH945-984	B6
75 (HP)	WJ564-582, 603-649, 674-682	B2
26	WJ712-734, 751-753	B2
31	WJ754-784	B6
11	WJ815-825	PR7
25	WJ857-881	T4
75 (A)	WJ971-995, WJ102-146, 161-165	B2
1	WN467	T4
2	WP514-515	B2
9 (S)	WT205-213	B6
6	WT301-306	B6
19	WT307-325	B(I) 6
30	WT326-348, 362-368	B(I) 8
6	WT369-374	B6
18	WT475-492	T4
40	WT503-542	PR7
1	WV787	B2
1	XA536	B2

1	XG554	B(I) 6
22 (S)	XH129-131, 133-137, 164-177	PR9
1	XH132	Short SC-9
25 (S)	XH203-209, 227-244	B(I) 8
4	XH567-570	B6
2	XH583-584	T4
2	XJ249, XJ257	B(I) 6
1	XK641	B6
2	XK647, XK650	T4
4	XK951-953, XK959	B(I) 8
20	XM244-245, 262-279	B(I) 8
1	XM936	B(I) 8

Total: 823 (822 Canberras, 1 SC-9; cancelled serials NOT included)

Note: Brackets indicate manufacturer other than EECo, ie S-Short; A-Avro; HP-Handley Page.

541	English Electric Co
132	Short (131 Canberras, 1 SC-9)
75	Avro
75	Handley Page
823	

EXPORTS

Australia

Type	Serial	Ex-RAF Serial	
B2	A84-1	WD935	but not delivered (remained RAF)
B2	A84-2	WH942	Remained on UK charge
B2	A84-3	WH710	Remained on UK charge
B2	A84-125	WD983	Converted T21
T4	A84-501	WT941	
T4	A84-502	WT492	
B2	A84-307	WD939	Converted T21

USA (Pattern Aircraft)

Serial	Ex-RAF Serial
51-17387	ex-WD932
51-17352	ex-WD940

France (Centre d'Essai En Vol)

Type	Serial	Ex-RAF Serial
B2	763	WJ763
B2	779	WJ779
B2	784	WJ784
B6	304	new

Venezuela

Type	1st serial	Ex-RAF	2nd serial	Class B for B52 conversion	Class B for B82 conversion	
B2	1A-39	WH708	—	—		W/off May 56
	1B-39	WH722	—	—		W/off Nov 54
	2A-39	WH709	6315	G27-159	G27-302	

B6	316	new
B6	318	new

Ecuador (all new B6s)

Serials: 801, 802, 803, 804, 805, 806

New Zealand

Type	Serial	Ex-RAF Serial
B12	NZ 6101	WT329
	NZ 6102-111	new
T13	NZ 6151	WD963
	NZ 6152	WE190

NB NZ survivors to India.

Sweden — Local designation Tp52

Type T11, serialled 52001 (ex-WH711), 52002 (ex-WH905)

South Africa

Type	Serial	Ex-RAF serial	
B12	451-456	new (456 — last production Canberra)	
T4	457	WJ991	
	458	WJ864	
	459	WJ617	

Type	1st Serial	Ex-RAF	2nd Serial	Class B for B52 conversion	Class B for B82 conversion
	2B-39	WH736	3246	G27-157	G27-309
	3A-39	WH729	6409	G27-158	G27-304
	3B-39	WH737	—	—	W/off Jan 63
				B(I)88 conversion	
B(I) 58	4A-39	XH244	3216	—	W/off Jan 69
	4B-39	new	0923	G27-308	(previous overhaul as G27-260)
	5A-39	new	—	—	W/off Apr 60
	5B-39	new			W/off Nov 64
	1C-39	new	0240	G27-254	
	2C-39	new	0269	G27-255	W/off Nov 78
	3C-39	new	0426	G27-256	
	4C-39	new	0453	G27-311	
				T84 conversion	
T54	1E-39	new	0619	G27-310	
	2E-39	new	0621	G27-265	
B52	0129	WH877		Converted B82 as	G27-301
	1131	WH647		B82	G27-257
	1183	WJ570		B82	G27-258
	1233	WF914		B82	G27-302
	1339	WH649		B82	G27-259
	1364	WD993		B82	G27-260
	1511	WH862		B82	G27-261
	2001	WJ980		B82	G27-262
B(I) 52	1280	WH881		Converted B(I) 82 as	G27-305
	1425	WH712		B(I) 82	G27-306
	1437	WH730		B(I) 82	G27-307
	1529	WH732/G27-3		B(I) 82	G27-263
PR53	2314	WEE172		Converted PR83 as	G27-264
	2444	WE171		—	W/off Mar 76

G27 serials replaced by original identity after re-delivery.

India

Type	Serial	Ex-RAF serial
B(I) 58	IF 895-913	XK953; XH203, 205; XK959; XH227, 229, 230, 232, 233, 235, 236; WT338; XH237, 238, 239, 240, 241, 242, 243
	IF 914-934	new (46)
	IF 960-984	
	BF 595-600	new (6)
PR57	IP 986-993	new (8)
	BP 745	ex-WT506
	BP 746	ex-WT539
T4	IQ 994	ex-XK647
	IQ 995	ex-XK650
	IQ 996-999	new (4)
	BQ 744	ex-... (WJ859?)
	Q495	ex-WH847 and G27-118 NOT delivered (diverted to Ethiopia)
	Q496	ex-WH845
	Q497	ex-WE191 and G27-116
	Q1791	ex-WE193

Type	Serial	Ex-RAF serial
	Q1792	ex-WE195
	Q1793	ex-WT485
	Q1794	ex-WT487
	Q1795	ex-WH839
	Q1796	ex-WJ868
B66	F1021	ex-WH954 and G27-167
	F1022	ex-WT210 and G27-168
	F1023	ex-WH959 and G27-177
	F1024	ex-WH961 and G27-178
	F1025	ex-? G27-174
	F1026	ex-? G27-172
	F1027	ex-? G27-173
	F1028	ex-WJ776 and G27-171
	F1029	ex-WJ303 and G27-170
	F1030	ex-WJ778 and G27-169

B12   Transferred *from New Zealand* (Nov-Dec 1970)
    F1183-1190   8 a/c (ex-NZ 6102, 6103, 6105, 6107, 6108, 6109, 6111 — sequence unknown)

T12   *ex-New Zealand*
    Q1191-1192   2 a/c (ex-NZ 6151 and 6152 — sequence unknown)

| T4 | P1098 | ex-RAF and G27-183 |
| | P1099 | ex-RAF and G27-184 |

West Germany (converted by Marshall of Cambridge)

ex-RAF	1st Serial	2nd Serial	3rd Serial	4th Serial
WK130	YA151	0001	D-9566	9936
WK137	YA152	0002	D-9567	9934
WK138	YA153	0003	D-9567	9935

Ethiopia (all B52s)

Serialled: 351 (ex-RAF), 352 (ex-RAF), 353 (ex-WJ857), 354 (ex-RAF)

Rhodesia/Zimbabwe

Type	ex-RAF	1st Serial	2nd Serial	3rd Serial
B2	WH867	159	200	2005
	WH653	160	201	2051
	WH662	161	202	2502
	WH672	162	203	5203
	WH707	163	204	2504
	WH855	164	205	2055
	WH871	165	206	2065
	WH883	166	207	Nil (W/off)
	WJ571	167	208	2085
	WJ572	168	209	2059
	WJ578	169	210	2510
	WJ606	170	211	Nil (W/off)
	WK108	171	212	Nil (W/off)
	WJ612	172	213	Nil (W/off)
	WH644	173	214	2514
T4	WH658	174	215	2155
	WH674	175	216	2156
	WJ613	176	217	2175
B2	WH666	in 1981	AFZ serials not yet known	
T4	WJ869	in 1981		

Peru

Type	Serial	Ex-RAF serial
B(I) 8	474	WT343
	475	WT348
	476	WT367
	478	XH206
	479-482	new (4)

One of the above crashed on 23 September 1956 and the seven survivors re-serialled 206-212, of which 208 was apparently also lost.

	208	replacement aircraft — new (1)
T4	231	WH659
	232	WJ860
	246	ex-RAF and G27-224
B2	233	WJ974 and G27-76
	234	WJ976 and G27-77
	235	WK112
	236	WH726
	237	WH868
	238	WE120
	239	WT208 and G27-96
	240	ex-G27-97
	241	ex-G27-98
	242	ex-G27-99
	243	G27-100
	244	G27-101
B(I) 8	245	WT344

Conversions by Marshall of Cambridge:

	247	WT368 and G52-2
	248	XK951 and G52-3
	249	WT342 and G52-4
	250	WT364 and G52-5
	251	WT340 and G52-6
	252	XH234 and G52-7
	253	XM273 and G52-8
	254	XM936 and G52-9
	255	XM263 and G52-10
	256	XM276 and G52-11
	257	XM278 and G52-12

Argentina

Type	Serial	Ex-RAF Serial	
B62	101	WJ616	G27-111/G-AYHO
	102	WJ714	G27-112/G-AYHP
	103	WJ713	G27-113
	104	WH913	G27-114
	105	WH702	G27-127
	106	ex-RAF	G27-165
	107	WH727	G27-162
	108	WH886	G27-164
	109	ex-RAF	G27-163
	110	ex-RAF	G27-166

Type	Serial	Ex-RAF Serial	
T64	111	WT476	G27-121
	112	WJ875	G27-122

2nd Order, 1981

B62		WH914
T64		XH583

CIVILIAN CANBERRAS

B2	G-ATZW	BAC Warton. First flew as civil aircraft 28 October 1966; retired 11 October 1967; ex-WD937.
PR57	VT-EEM	National Remote Sensing Agency, Secundrabad, India. Registered July 1976. Ex-IAF (serial unknown).

RAF CONVERSIONS

WD/WE Batch

Converted to	Serial
T4	WD944, 954, 963, WE111
U10	WD951, 961
U14	WD941
T17	WD955
TT18	WE122

WF Batch

T17	WF980, 916

WH Batch

T4	WH637, 651, 658, 659, 674, 706, 854, 861
U10	WH714, 724, 903, 904 all later T19
U14	WH704, 720, 876, 921 (876 back to B2)
B15	WH947, 948, 954-961, 963-974, 977, 981, 983, 984 of which WH 948, 957, 964, 972, 973, 981, 983 converted to E15 and WH961 to PR16
T17	WH646, 664, 665, 740, 863, 872, 874, 902
TT18	WH718, 856, 887
PR9	WH793 — prototype
T22	WH780, 797, 801, 803

WJ Batch

T4	WJ566, 568, 613, 617
B2T	WJ681
B6RC	WJ768, 775
B(I) 8	WJ643
U10/D10	WJ604, 621, 623, 624
T11	WJ610, 734 (WJ610 to T19)
U14-D14	WJ638
B15	WJ756, 760, 762, 764, 766 (756 to E15)
B16	WJ770, 771, 773, 774, 776, 777, 778, 780-783

T17	WJ565, 576, 581, 607, 625, 630, 633				
TT18	WJ754, 614, 629, 632, 636, 639, 680, 682, 715, 717, 721				

WJ/WK Batch

T4	WJ991, 992
U10	WJ987, WK107, 110
T11	WJ975, WK106 both to T19
T17	WJ977, 981, 986, 988, WK102, 111
TT18	WK118, 122, 123, 124, 126, 127, 142
B2E	WK164

WT Batch

B15	WT205, 208, 209, 210, 211, 213
B16	WT302, 303, 306, 369, 372, 373, 374
B6RC	WT206, WT305
B6	WT327, 333
T22	WT510, 525, 535

XA Batch

T11 then T19	XA536

XH Batch

B16	XH570

XK Batch

B15	XK641

RAF AND ROYAL NAVY OVERHAUL CONTRACT

In order of arrival at Samlesbury

WK116	B2	Arrived 2/6/76. Returned to RAF 3/7/78

WJ678	B2		WH646	T17
WH849	T4		WT519	PR7
WK111	T17		WJ861	T4
WT480	T4		WK126	TT18
WP515	B2		WK118	TT18
WJ879	T4		WH718	TT18
WH887	TT18		WJ633	T17
WK127	TT18		WH972	E15
WK162	B2		WK142	TT18
WD955	T17		WH983	E15
WJ981	T17		WJ682	TT18
WT509	PR7		WH779	PR7
WK124	TT18		WT478	T4
WJ715	TT18		WJ625	T17
WH981	E15		WJ874	T4
WJ986	T17		WH902	T17
WJ636	TT18		WF890	T17
WJ731	B2		WF916	T17
WJ877	T4		WJ717	TT18
WT538	PR7		WJ574	TT18
WH664	T17		WJ680	TT18
WH670	B2		WJ630	T17
WJ756	E15		WK123	TT18
WE113	B2		WJ866	T4
WJ607	T17		WJ614	TT18
WH848	T4		WE122	TT18
WJ567	B2			

3 Air Force and other Users

Royal Air Force
Royal Navy
Ministry of Defence (Procurement Executive)
Royal Aircraft Establishment

Country	Date of first delivery	Country	Date of first delivery
Argentina	11 November 1970	Peru	25 May 1956
Australia (mostly built under licence)		Rhodesia/Zimbabwe	5 May 1959
		South Africa	19 October 1963
Ecuador	20 May 1955	Sweden	January 1960
Ethiopia	28 July 1968	Taiwan	
France	4 August 1955	(supplied from USA)	
Federal Republic of Germany	14 September 1966	United States (built under licence)	
India	1 April 1957	Venezuela	3 March 1952
New Zealand	?? ????? 1960		
Pakistan (supplied from USA)			

4   Canberra Records

Date	Journey	Time
12/2/51	Aldergrove-Gander	4hr 37min (unofficial)
1-4/8/51	UK-Darwin	21hr 41min (unofficial)
31/8/51	Aldergrove-Gander	4hr 18min 24.4sec
18/2/52	London-Tripoli	2hr 41min 49.5sec
26/8/52	Aldergrove-Gander and return	10hr 3min 29.28sec
	Gander-Aldergrove	3hr 25min 18.13sec
28/9/52	London-Nairobi	9hr 55min 16.7sec
27/1/53	London-Karachi	8hr 52min 28.2sec
27-28/1/53	London-Darwin	22hr 21.8sec
4/5/53	World altitude record of 63,668ft	
8/10/53	London-Basra	5hr 11min 5.6sec
8-9/10/53	London-Christchurch, New Zealand	23hr 50min 42sec
8-9/10/53	London-Colombo	10hr 25min 21.5sec
17/12/53	London-Capetown	12hr 21min 3.8sec
19/12/53	Capetown-London	13hr 16min 25.2sec
27-28/6/55	Ottawa-London	6hr 42min 12sec
23/8/55	London-New York	7hr 29min 56.7 sec
	New York-London	6hr 16min 59.5sec
	London-New York-London	14hr 21min 45.5sec
29/8/53	World altitude record of 65,890ft	
16/2/56	London-Cairo	3hr 57min 18.9sec
25/5/57	Tokyo-London	17hr 42min 2.4sec
28/8/57	World altitude record of 70,310ft	
22/2/58	Washington DC-Caracas	4hr 10min 59.7sec

5   Key Personnel

Following the departure of Petter and some of his team in 1950 many hundreds of people continued working on the project under Page, and some of those in key positions were:

In Design

Don Crowe	Chief Engineer
B. O. (Ollie) Heath	Chief of Stress
Dai Ellis	Wind Tunnels
Ray Creasey	Aerodynamics
Ron Dickson	Aerodynamics
John King	Mechanical Test
Roland Coles	Mechanical Test
Ted Loveless	Stress
Bill Gornal	Stress
C. F. Wills	Design Office
F. Bradford	Design Office
Bill Mars	Design Office
Cliff Tarr	Electrical Design
Peter Kubicki	Weights
Fred Holden	Weights

Barbara Barton	Tracing
Bill Walker	Administration
Bill Moran	Technical Publications
Bob Hothersall	Warton Airfield Superintendent
Bill Eaves	Warton Flight Sheds Superindent
Joe Sarginson	Design/Works Liaison
Glen Hobday	Design Office and later EE Co representative at Glen L. Martin, USA
Mike Cara	Aerodynamics, and later Manager, Canberra Programme
Gordon Whitely	Flight Test Engineer
Derek Hargreaves	Flight Test Engineer

Canberra Test Aircrew under R. P. Beamont
1949-54
Pilots: J. W. C. Squier, Peter Hillwood, T. Evans, P. Laurence, J. Still, R. Whittington. Navigator: Denis Watson.

Joining after 1954

Pilots: D. de Villiers, Tim Ferguson, John Hall, Keith Isherwood, Don Knight, John Cockburn, John Hackett (ferry pilot), Eric Bucklow.

Navigators: Peter Moneypenny, Jim Evans, Brian McCann, Ray Woolett.

Works personnel under Arthur Sheffield, Works Manager Preston

Jimmy Rowe	Production Superintendent
Bob Hollock	Manager, Experimental Shop
Cliff Eastwood	Works Inspection (Quality Control)
Stan Jackson	Plating Department
Fred Maidment	Superintendent of Progress

George Walker	Superintendent, Samlesbury Flight Shed
John Crowther	Aircraft Service Department (also in charge of the ground support of every major Canberra display at Farnborough and overseas from 1949 to 1969)
W. Shorrock	Asst Works Manager
Jimmy Hanmer	Production Superintendent

Government representatives

Hugh Howatt	Resident Technical Officer, MoS
'Wilky' Wilkinson	AID Inspector, MoS

6 Canberras 'refurbished' for Export

Mark	Number	Serials	Delivered	Remarks
Rhodesia				
B2	15	RRAF 159-173	3-6/59	Ex-RAF direct, not through EE
T4	3	RRAF 174-176	3/61	Converted from B2 to T4 by EE before delivery
Sweden				
Tp 52	2	52001, 52002	Spring 1960	B2 a/c ex-RAF converted by Boulton-Paul/EE to TR11 standard (but no radar fitted)
South Africa				
T4	3	457-459	Spring 1964	T4 a/c ex-RAF overhauled by BAC before delivery
West Germany				
B2	3	YA 151-153	9-12/66	Overhauled by Marshall's before delivery through BAC
Ethiopia				
B52	4	351-354	7-11/68	B2 a/c ex-RAF converted and refurbished by BAC
Argentina				
B62	10	B101-110	11/70 to 9/71	B2 and T4 a/c ex-RAF converted and refurbished by BAC
T64	2	B111-112	9/71	
Peru				
B2	6	233-238	8/66-12/67	ex-RAF a/c refurbished by BAC
T4	2	231, 232	4-5/66	
B(I)56	6	239-244	2/69-6/69	ex-RAF B2 and B6 a/c converted and refurbished by BAC
B(I)68	1	245	7/71	Ex-RAF B(I)8 a/c converted and refurbished by BAC
T4	1	246	2/73	Ex-RAF a/c, refurbished by BAC, originally for India, but delivered to Peru

Mark	Number	Serials	Delivered	Remarks
B(I)68	8	247-254	3/75-1/76	Ex-RAF B(I)8 a/c, converted and refurbished by Marshall's; limited work by BAC
B(I)68	3	255-257	10/77-7/78	

Venezuela

Mark	Number	Serials	Delivered	Remarks
B2	12	0129, 1131, 1183, 1233, 1280, 1339, 1364, 1425, 1437, 1511, 1529, 2001	12/65 to 4/67	Ex-RAF aircraft refurbished by BAC
PR3	2	2314, 2444	8, 10/66	
B2	(3)	3246, 6315, 6409	5-8/69	Refurbished by BAC, originally delivered new to Venezuela in 1953 (B2) and 1957 (B(I))
B(I)8	(1)	0923	4/71	
B82	(15)			Refurbished by BAC, all Venezuelan aircraft delivered new in 1953 or 1957, or refurbished in 1969-71
PR 83	(1)			
T84	(2)	various	7/77 to 5/80	
B(I)88	(5)			

India

Mark	Number	Serials	Delivered	Remarks
T4	1	BQ 744	9/63	Ex-RAF T4 overhauled by BAC before delivery
PR 57	2	BP 745, 746	Spring 1964	Ex-RAF PR7 converted and overhauled by BAC
T4	1+(2)	Q495, 496, 497	1 A/c 8/68	Ex-RAF T4 a/c, delivery embargoed in 1966. Only Q495 ever delivered
B(I)66	10	IF 1020-1029	1970	Ex-RAF B15/B16
PR 67	2	IP 1098, 1099	1971	Ex-RAF PR7; both refurbished by BAC
T4	6	Q1791-1796	Mid-1975	Ex-RAF T4 a/c, direct from RAF St Athan. Not handled by BAC
B(I)12	8	not known	Late 1970	ex-RNZAF a/c, sold to India.
T13				

7   Bibliography

British Aerospace, Warton, Archives.
Bombers of the West; Gunston.
The British Bomber Since 1914; Lewis.
Flying Logbook; Beamont.
Flying Logbook; Squier.
Notes on English Electric Aviation; Ransome and Fairclough.
Aviation Week and Space Technology; Hotz.
Flight International.
British Aerospace, Hatfield, Archives.
Report, Napier Scorpion Rocket; Shirley.
Imperial War Museum, Photo Archives.
Notes on Serial Nos; P. A. Jackson.
Air Pictorial.

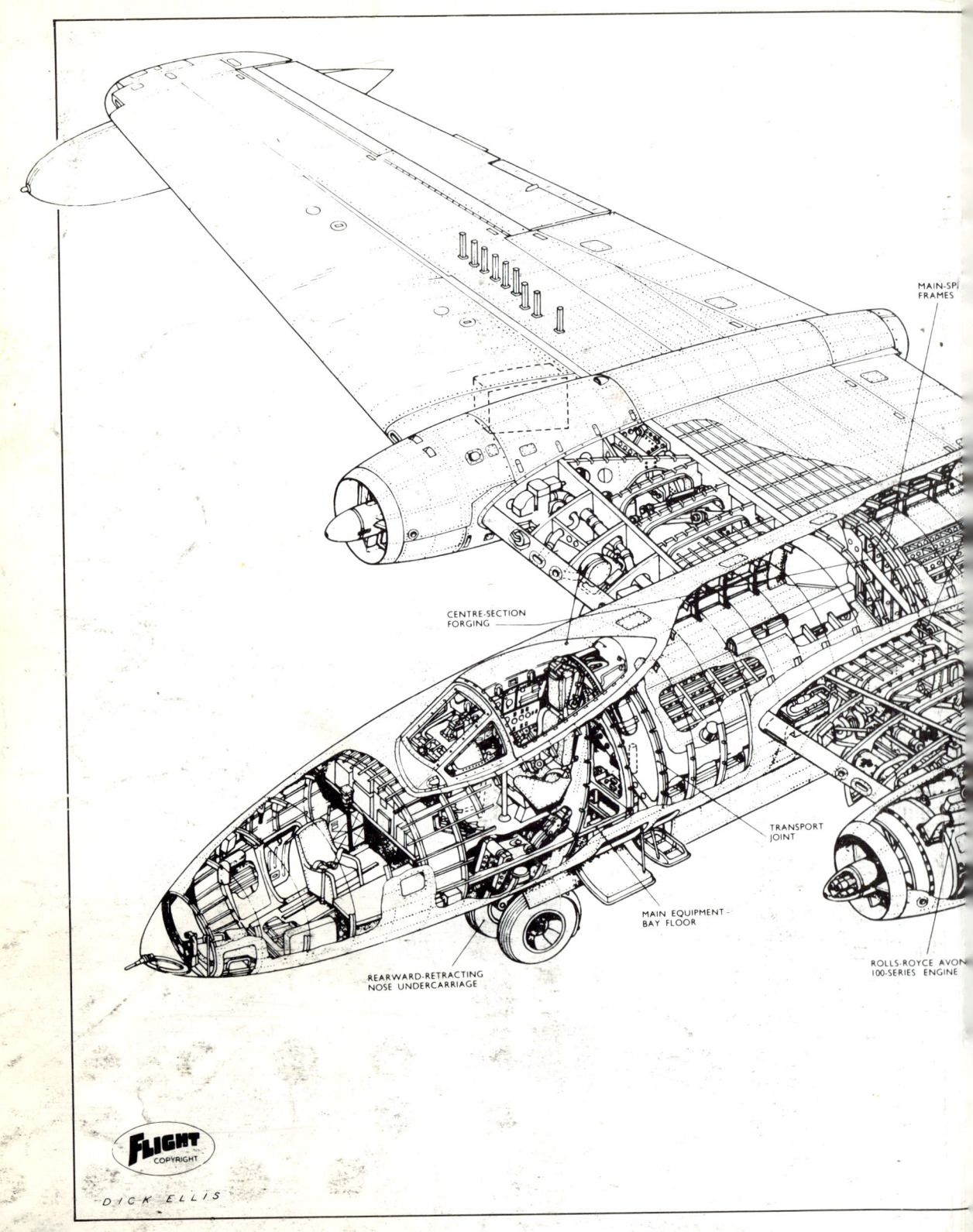

MAIN-SP/
FRAMES

CENTRE-SECTION
FORGING

TRANSPORT
JOINT

MAIN EQUIPMENT-
BAY FLOOR

ROLLS-ROYCE AVON
100-SERIES ENGINE

REARWARD-RETRACTING
NOSE UNDERCARRIAGE